I'm On Your Side…
Scoot Over

Every Marriage Desires More

The FUN Marriage Collection

Joe Woodruff

I'm On Your Side... Scoot Over

To Natalie

"Sincerely Yours"

I'm On Your Side...Scoot Over

Contents

I'm On Your Side...Scoot Over

Have Fun. Seriously

I sit on a balcony with the Mediterranean before me. Islands dot the landscape. Sand walkways bid me to the beach, palm trees lining the path. To my left, a cliff is crowned by an ancient house of worship. The sea itself glistens with blues and greens. Natural beauty ascends imagination. It is a landscape I do not see every day.

Behind me, a greater beauty stands in my bedroom. She is unclothed. Her delicate features are freshly washed. Hair still damp, it frames eyes that draw me and lips that fascinate me. Soft and rounded shoulders perch above her petite and slender frame. I instinctively move toward her, as I have since the first I saw her.

In the spring of 1980, I stood in the front of a room talking with a friend. Many of our high school peers were gathering, taking places in chairs. I glanced up as she walked in. I said, "Look at her!" As she sat in the center of an aisle, my friend and I ran to opposite sides and threw ourselves into the seats next to her.

After that day, I took advantage of any opportunity to talk with her. Six months later she agreed to a date. Thirteen months after that we were engaged to be married.

Now for over thirty years, I see her most every day. Her beauty refreshes me. As she reaches to begin to dress, I ask her if she must. She smiles knowingly.

Baby, I'm Amazed By You

An ancient poet describes the way of a man with a woman as too amazing for him.
Amazing depicts the wonderful and the incomprehensible. Amazing was used by early writers to portray the artistry of God.

We crave amazing. The look of someone's eyes that hold you in place; the first brush of hands and the assuring lock of fingers; an evening that leaves you laughing even after its end. We long for the first kiss that is beyond equal, the kiss where sensations and wonder crash with welcome disorientation. And we seek the second kiss that somehow eclipses the first, spiced with a little more confidence and a lot more invitation.

Infatuation is welcomed and makes itself at home with love. When ancients spoke of the *way* of a man and woman, they referred to actions occurring over time. Amazing is not bound by one moment or event alone. Amazing is ageless.

The same poet also describes the tragic: an unloved person who is married. He says it is similar to the earth trembling under a weight it cannot bear. We have seen this too:

> Looks that caused the heart to melt,
> Kisses that sent the spirit soaring,
> Fingers entwined symbolic of heart;
> All now memories of a time long past,
> Relics of two who have grown apart.

You are intended for amazing not for abandoned.

Your Marriage Is Made For FUN

Every marriage desires more. A solid marriage desires greater depths and higher heights. A crumbling marriage seeks to recapture what was lost. No marriage wants to just move past problems. They want to move into the promise that stirred its beginning.

The marriage you desire is FUN. In it, each person experiences what it means to be:

- Free: You are loved for who you are, as you are, to become all you are.
- United: You are loved with unbridled passion without fear of separation or failure.
- New: You are loved through life's changes and together you change life.

You can feel this. You know instinctively it is true. Marriage isn't an institution to live up to, it's a relationship to live into. Marriage doesn't come with a blueprint to erect but with a design to experience. And that design is for each person to know with their partner what it means to be free, united and new.

Adam and Eve had a pretty famous marriage. It was an arranged marriage. Can you imagine if they tried to find each other through an online dating service? "Your search has returned 1 of 1 match." Adam had the easiest pick-up line ever: "Ta-dah!" Their first date had no dress code and consisted of spare ribs for dinner followed by a karaoke duet of *It Had To Be You*.

God breathed into Adam the breath of life. *Breath* means you have a future to realize. You do not lose your best self in marriage. On the contrary, you are joined by a partner who refuses to see you held back and whose love is driven to surface your best. You and your partner are free.

Adam and Eve became one flesh. *One* pictures what is knit together and distinct. You are no longer two people others know, you are a couple. People don't' think of one without the other. There is another with whom you share a new identity.

Adam described their identity as "bone of my bone and flesh of my flesh." As one, you experience physical and emotional bonding. To be free does not mean self-sufficient. You are created to be connected. You are intended to depend on each other for physical need and emotional health. You are united.

God blessed Adam and Eve and told them to fill the earth. To *fill* means to furnish. How cool is that! Together you furnish what would not otherwise be. You are made new and you make new.

This is the marriage you desire. Each contending for your mate's true self, you are irresistible to the other and inseparable. No matter what life brings, you shape it to the fullness for which your marriage is designed. And the world is better because of it.

When Marriage Is Not FUN

How does amazing love turn into abandoned love? How does passion pale? How are two in love lonely?

Adam and Eve began their relationship naked and unashamed. Then they turned away from God and tried to make sense of life on their own. They failed. Afterwards, God walked in the garden and asked, "Where are you?" That was a very sad day. For the first time in human history, distance was felt. One became several.

Adam and Eve were *afraid*. As a result, they *hid*. Then they *covered* their bodies. They were no longer naked and unashamed. Their relationship fractured.

Fear rooted in shame causes separation.

Shame is a distorted conviction of your worth, belonging and competence. It is the belief that you are deeply flawed: unworthy, unacceptable and unable. You believe it is only a matter of time until you will be found out and judged.

Fear is both immediate and underlying. We can be frightened in a moment. We can dread something over time. We fear the real and the imagined, the known and the unknown. At the heart of fear is concern for our well-being. We fear that people will not value us. We dread rejection. We cringe at failure.

Hiding and covering is the behavior of fear rooted in shame. To protect our well-being, we hide from people what could cause them to punish us or leave us. We cover our own insecurity in disguises of criticism and control.

Fear and shame is a vicious cycle. Our fear of disconnection and our shame in disappointment energize the cycle until, if unchecked, it spins out of control.

She fears distance in the relationship is worsening. She thinks about it a lot, and the more she thinks the more she worries. She tries to talk to her husband but he avoids conversations. He is afraid he has disappointed her. Talking about his concerns will only expose his failure. The more she wants to talk about it, the more he wants to avoid talking. The more he avoids, the more she worries.

"His shame is too great to allow him to understand her fear and her fear keeps her from seeing his shame (Dr. Patricia Love, *How To Improve Your Marriage Without Talking About It*)."

The problem is we enter marriage with ideals and images. They have been formed as we watched other marriages build or fall apart. They have been informed by what we have heard or read. Marriage then becomes an entity in itself that we try to realize or perfect. It comes with rules and principles. Now my worth, belonging and competence is measured by a standard or a model. My performance is on the line. Marriage becomes something I must live up to. In this, it does nothing but feed fear and shame.

But marriage isn't an institution to live up to, it's a relationship to live into.

In marriage, you will disagree. You will have different preferences. Your interests will not always sync. Words will be spoken you wish you could take back. Bad attitudes will need correction. Someone will do something stupid. Grumpy will wake up. Nothing in your marriage – family, finances, friendships, faith or sex – will always be the way you want. And none of them will be the core issue at the heart of any problem. Your real problem will not be a poor financial plan or conflict in communication or boredom in the bedroom.

The core issues are:

- Is someone's sense of worth being validated or threatened? Does a person feel free and able to thrive or do they feel bound?

- Is someone's sense of belonging being strengthened or challenged? Do they feel united or do they feel pushed away?

- Is someone's sense of competence being promoted or diminished? Do they feel new and limitless or do they feel stuck?

At the heart of every FUN marriage is deep friendship. "This is my lover, this is my friend" declares the Beloved in the Song of Songs. As friends, we guard and encourage each other's worth, belonging and competence.

When Adam was alone, God said it was not good. We think of alone as *by his self*, but there is a deeper meaning to the word alone.

God made for Adam a helper, Eve. The word *helper* is used elsewhere to describe God. It captures his activity to rescue and be victorious. It is not a word that means subordinate or inferior. Hebrew had four other words for helper and each of them denote subordination. None of those words are used in the account of Adam and Eve.

A helper is an agent of God in the life of another. To be alone means you are not in a relationship in which God is using a person to help you. You can surround yourself with people and still be alone if none of them are contending with you to overcome fear and shame. God wants to deliver everyone from fear and shame. He did so in Jesus. He continues to do so through people.

Marriage is the relationship in which fear and shame is defeated and worth, belonging and competence is promoted.

Marriage is not defined by roles and rules, commitment and covenant, communication and compromise. I didn't marry a covenant, I married a person. I didn't marry a commitment, I married a partner. I don't fulfill a role but I do love a unique individual with different needs at different times. Compromise does not define selfless. My communication isn't about understanding or being understood, it's about affirming, accepting and advocating for this person I am crazy in love with and hope that when I breathe my last I do so lying next to them.

In this crazy love, I am committed and make covenant. I give and I take. I assume roles and adopt helpful rules. I do communicate. But marriage isn't about that. Those dynamics serve my marriage, they don't define my marriage.

Marriage is a relationship you live into because love is focused on a person. It is consumed with that person. You serve that person, not because of some standard you're trying to meet but because someone whose best interest compels you. Anything short of that isn't love; it's law. And you can live a lot of law and never know love.

Your marriage was made for amazing love.

Move Toward Hope

The following chapters explore what it means to be free, united and new in marriage.

You will be free. You will learn how to affirm in ways that is meaningful to the other, how to communicate acceptance and what it means to be an advocate for your partner.

You will be united. You will embrace the mystery of how two are one and yet one is more than two. You will understand what it means to communicate deep needs and identify threat. You will capture greater and more intimate expressions of romance and sex.

You will be new. You will learn to identify right change for your marriage and you will understand how to rally, shape and drive transformation in your marriage.

You desire more. You will experience more.

In the *I Love Lucy* episode "Vacation from Marriage" Lucy and her husband, Ricky are in the room with their two married friends, Fred and Ethel.

Lucy: Our lives have become a stale routine. We do the same thing in the same way. We know each other like a book.

Ricky: Well, honey, that's only normal. After you're married for 11 years, you're supposed to know each other like a book.

Fred: It's the same after 25 years, only their cover gets more dog-eared.

Lucy: Do you realize we're in a terrible rut? We have become stuffy, moldy and musty. We are knee-deep in a pool of stagnation. Now what are we going to do about it?

Fred: Well, I don't know about the rest of you, but I'm gonna go and take a shower.

At the end of the episode, after trying to take a week away from each other, Lucy says to Ricky, "I don't want a vacation from marriage. I'd rather be in a rut with you."

It's a sweet episode, but I have a better idea.

The Hebrews believed that he who married obtained favor from God. God told them to enjoy life with their wife for this is their reward before heaven. Early followers of Jesus were taught "Let marriage be held in honor." The word honor was used to describe items that were costly and precious. Its origin is from the word time. The value of something is seen over time or may be as valuable as time itself. Once time is lost you can never retrieve it; time well-spent gives back for generations.

Favor. Reward. Honor.

Marriage is not a worn book so read it is all too familiar.

Marriage is the altar of your worship.

Marriage is the visible display of your heart's desire and the gift you offer God. "If you want to honor me," God says, "Show me in your marriage."

Seriously FUN

I take my wife's hand and we stroll along the beach. The ocean before us is vast but waves and tides are a common sight to God's eyes. Marriage never fails to touch his heart.

As our feet mix in with the sand, we walk an unknown path. Recent days have seen troubled times. Our words of encouragement and our prayers of faith have sustained us while people we trusted have failed us. The confidence in our step even with the questions in our heart rises as worship.

I think about the night before. Our bodies moved in rhythm. Eyes were shut in pleasure and opened in sensation. I held her to me as her breath released in exquisite relief, our sighs of satisfaction rising as hymns in heaven.

I return to the present. Back in our room, I read a great mystery while she writes down recipes. It's something we have done for years. I've read more books than I can remember, and she's recorded more recipes than she has time or inclination to cook. But oneness knows many expressions. The daily is a colorful thread in the tapestry of God's marital handiwork.

The tapestry hasn't been without stain or tear. My wife and I have had our trials. We have suffered heartbreak and bitter loss. Depression couldn't down us and disappointment couldn't drown us. Misunderstanding got in the way but forgiveness got it out of the way. Debt nearly sunk us and best laid plans almost buried us. We have risen to challenges and we have bowed to fights we couldn't win. In all, if not perfectly, we have been together. We are free. We are united. We are new. And God is pleased.

You don't need a vacation from marriage. But you also don't need to live in a rut. Not when amazing is before you.

The FUN Coach

To be free means to be loved for who you are and as you are to become all you are. To be united is to be loved with unbridled passion without fear of separation or failure. To be new is to be loved through life's changes and together change life for the better.

Let's just do an easy check-in for now:

1. In what ways do you currently feel free? What does not feel free?

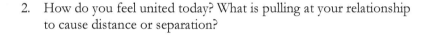

2. How do you feel united today? What is pulling at your relationship to cause distance or separation?

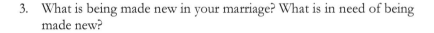

3. What is being made new in your marriage? What is in need of being made new?

Shame gives root to fear which acts out in behavior. Each relate to areas of worth, belonging and competence. Worth has to do with qualities *inherent* in us. Belonging addresses the *interaction* we have with people. Competence is concerned with our *ideas and intentions*.

Review the following chart. Shame believes lies, fears certain outcomes and exhibits itself in harmful behavior.

Shame: Worth	Fear: Worth	Behavior: Worth
Defective	Judgment	Hide or withdraw
Inferior	Used and abused	Hurt myself
Fake	Found Out	Boasting or denial
Not Valued	Ignored, Unappreciated	Criticism
Disrespectable	Looking bad	Fix on my own
	Misunderstanding	Justify
	Disliked	Accusation, Sarcasm
		Manipulation, Control
		Secretive

Shame: Belonging	Fear: Belonging	Behavior: Belonging
Unlovable	Love will not last	Question and distrust
Unwanted	Rejection	Snoop
Controlled	Abandonment	Jealousy
Disconnected	Rumor	Anger
Lonely	Neglect	Project and judge motive
	Mistrust	Group or isolate
	Ridicule	Cling, Hover
		Avoid conflict

Shame: Competence	Fear: Competence	Behavior: Competence
Unable, Incapable	Blame, fault	Blame, find fault
Stupid	Disappointment	Cover up
Helpless, powerless	Complaint, criticism	Try harder or not try at all
A Failure	Failure	Anger
Inadequate	Invalidated	Boast, lie
		Passive-aggressive
		Fix

Control

1. As you review the list, identify the one or two beliefs, fears and behaviors that surface most frequently in your life. (For example, someone might write: I believe I am not valued and unwanted. I fear judgment and rejection. I am secretive and try to fix things on my own).

2. Note one or two points of shame, fear and behaviors that are not issues you wrestle with.

3. Think about a most recent problem, whether in any relationship or situation. Can you see how a lie or a fear motivated your responses?

4. Look again at the one or two beliefs and fears that seem prominent for you. In your heart and mind, label them "enemy." We will come back to this idea later.

I Sleep With 365 Women A Year

I sleep with the woman who toasts each New Year with me. She has a bubbly personality.

I sleep with the woman who sees what I look like first thing in the morning. She is an optimist.

I sleep with the woman who birthed three amazing children. She is a saint in need of a nap.

I sleep with the woman who prays us through every challenge. She wears knee pads.

Some nights I sleep with Jasmine, the daring Princess. She is strong and fierce and adventurous. Many nights I sleep with Belle who finds love for the Beast in me. Once in a while, I sleep with Snow White. She loves my dopey side. Often I sleep with Cinderella whose simple origins and dainty feet capture my heart and make me feel like a prince. There are even nights I sleep with Cruella Deville, especially after our dog has made a doggone mess where she shouldn't have. Cruella is hot!

In the Song of Songs, an ancient love poem, the Lover tells his Beloved she has hair like a flock of goats, a nose like the tower of Lebanon and a neck like the tower of David. If you ever drew a picture to match his description you'd think twice about uploading it to your online album. Somehow she took it all as a compliment. I suspect what was important to her wasn't the description itself but the details he noticed and delighted in.

You married a person with a zillion incredible qualities. If you think about him as a movie star, you might see how he is like a suave James Bond, an adventurous Indiana Jones, a well-intentioned Inspector Clouseau, a playful Ferris Bueller or a sexy, confident Denzel Washington. (Please don't tell me you thought of Dumb and Dumber. Not affirming). If you think about her as a wonder of the world, you will find in her the mystery of the pyramids, the lush colors of the Babylonian gardens and the grandeur of the cavernous canyon.

How well do you see your partner? Do you see their value, their attraction and qualities that others seek and approve of? Are you aware of their commitment, comfort and support, their affection and trust? Do you recognize their competence, success and significance?

Proverbs say a wife of noble character is worth far more than rubies. King Solomon wrote a wife of noble character is her husband's crown. He contrasted her with a disgraceful wife who is like decay in his bones (Solomon knew a thing or two about wives. He had 700).

The word disgrace means one who puts to shame. The word noble describes virtue, honor and strength. It's an interesting contrast. We can be a partner who acting out of our shame puts another to shame, or we can be a partner who in our nobility recognizes the nobility of the other.

It's a critical difference.

Mirror, Mirror

In the classic tale of Snow White, the wicked stepmother asks her magic mirror on the wall, "Who is the fairest of them all?" One day the mirror responded, "Not you."

There are mirrors that make you look fatter or thinner, taller or shorter. We are surrounded by different mirrors called people. We see reflections of who we are through their clarity or distortion. Look into a distorted mirror and you suffer a distorted self-image.

When Adam and Eve failed, history says their eyes were opened and they realized they were naked. Their perception changed. They saw each other in terms of their differences. Their shame convinced them that different is bad. In response, they covered up. For the first time, being different was a point of fear instead of a point of favor. Has anyone used something that is different about you as a basis of judgment?

Blame and rejection followed. Inequality and lack of appreciation set in. God warned Eve that her desire would be for Adam, but that Adam would choose to rule over her. *Rule over* means to control. Control was not a part of God's original design.

When Eve first gave birth, she said, "With the help of the Lord I have brought forth a man." I think Adam had something to do with it too. Some would say, "She was just giving ultimate credit to the giver of life." I'm not so sure. Another time she said, "God granted me another child." Each time she gave birth, she named the child. Up until then, Adam had named every living thing, including Eve.

Adam probably thought Eve didn't appreciate him. Eve didn't feel treated as an equal. Even though they lived for years together and produced many children, they reinforced each other's fear and shame. They lived in a house of distorted mirrors.

God has made your marriage to be home to equality and appreciation. Blame and rejection has no place in paradise. You can be naked and unashamed. You can be free. You can be loved for who you are and as you are so as to become all God designed.

Free begins with affirmation. You are your partner's mirror. You see and reflect the qualities of their worth, belonging and competence. They have enemies: lies, fears and behaviors that you help vanquish.

Do you know your partner's enemies? They need you to expose those lies and reinforce the truth of what they need not fear and of what behaviors need no longer trap them.

How well do you see them? What do you reflect to them?

Two Reflections

A doctor named Luke told a true story with three central characters:

- Pharisee: A religious specialist.
- Jesus: God who became man. Miracle birth. Miracle worker.
- Woman: A professional sex worker

Jesus accepted a dinner invitation at the house of the Pharisee. The woman crashed the party. Cultural rules allowed for this. You can watch. You may only eat leftovers.

The woman brought with her a jar of perfume. Perfume came in many forms including scented balms and oils. Alabaster jars were highly prized. She stood behind the feet of Jesus who was reclining at the table in order to eat. She wept and her tears wet his feet. She wiped his feet with her hair, kissed them repeatedly and poured perfume on them.

This woman had let her hair down many times with plenty of men but not as an act of love. Her lips had kissed others but never with such heart.

The two men reacted differently.

The Pharisee said to himself, but loud enough to be heard, "If this man is who he says, he would know that the woman touching him is a sinner." The religious specialist mirrored her past actions and held them forth as a basis for rejection. His distorted perception communicated "your life is wrong and you do not belong."

Jesus affirmed her. Jesus, who lived a pure and sinless life in selfless generosity, was approachable and touchable. He let his feet be kissed over and over by this woman. If you move past the initially awkward you realize it is incredibly tender. Some would consider the action to be more fitting for lovers behind closed doors. Jesus welcomed her.

Jesus spoke forgiveness to her, refusing to allow the condemnation of the religious specialist to reinforce her fear and shame. Forgiveness sets a person free from the binds of fear and shame.

Then Jesus said, "Go in peace." Peace means to be whole. Peace means you are in one piece as opposed to broken to pieces. "Go as one I see as whole," Jesus says.

Jesus applauded an inner beauty complementary to her outer beauty. He assured her she belonged. He ensured that her act of worship would be made known throughout the world.

Jesus affirmed the beauty of her life and the meaning of her life. We do the same to affirm our partner.

Snowed White

The Bible, which is a book about relationships, is full of references to beauty. Daughters were called beautiful. A woman named Rachel is described as lovely in form and beautiful. The Song of Songs is filled with references to beauty (even beauty like goats). One woman noticed the beauty of Joseph. She was married and he was not. She made the play, and when he refused, she made him pay.

Beauty isn't only physical. Ancients wrote of the beauty of the inward spirit.

The word beauty described something that was better or best. It referred to what was favored and precious. The word was even used to describe being at ease. Picture a lounge chair on a sunny beach with no worries in the world…beautiful.

You meet a person and qualities set them apart from others. They are better to you and they become the best for you. Given the choice, you prefer their company over someone else. You value what they possess more than what any other can bring. You are able to be more relaxed, more yourself.

Andre Maurois wrote "All love begins with an impact."

Physical features capture you. Their laughter energizes you. Thoughtfulness touches you. You catch your lover talking sweetly to a child. They don't realize you are watching as they help a stranger. Twisted humor fits with yours. You both believe music can never be too loud and tattoos can never be too much. Your lover's preference for a peaceful evening at home is heaven to you. Their soft touch and taste of their lips is like no other.

Love that began with impact transformed into influence. You are better and at your best because of your partner. Their beauty is beheld in the exhibits of the personal, the social and the spiritual: the attraction of their body and mind, the appeal of their interactions, the charisma of their influence.

You are mesmerized by their physical pull on you, like a gravitational force. Eyes look into you more than they look at you. Hair frames the face and scents the pillow: styled, it sparks your imagination; messed, it amuses your memory. The kiss of their lips rises above the mundane and races you to lands of more. The hold of their hands is security and assurance; their touch is familiar and tantalizing at the same time.

You crave the opportunity to place your hand upon his chest as if the strength of his frame that shields his heart protects your very own. Her breasts draw your eyes and enflames your desire. Arms and legs and delights in-between possess you and are like art that once seen can never be seen enough.

Surveys indicate that what both men and women desire most in their marriage is communication. Yes, men too. Friendship is built and enriched on exchanges of thought and wit.

Your lover sees and thinks and imagines and dreams and plans and does. Their beliefs stimulate and intrigue; their insight changes or catalyzes your own. Their convictions are foundations of assurance and points of a compass. You cry at their reflections, laugh at their word play, sail upon their encouragement, move forward on their resolve. The work of their hands is so good others take it for granted. Skill long-learned looks easy; words are crafted, fingers dance, voice hums. How is your lover beautiful in body and mind?

Marriage lives in the lives of others. Your partner has a way with people. Their compassion touches your heart. Their leadership inspires you. As they serve others, you are pulled to give more of yourself. If they are an extrovert, you love their buoyant personality and their ability to engage the world around them. If they are an introvert, you long to explore the experiences they are processing. People seek out the one you love; they applaud their accomplishments and mourn their absence. Famed or behind the scenes, they matter to hearts other than your own but never more than your own. How is your lover beautiful to others?

Marriage lives in the seen and unseen, the tangible and the intangible, the natural and the spiritual. All that you admire in body and mind, interaction and skill matters. Your lover influences the world around them and the world beyond them. Their faith guides you. Their hope strengthens and inspires you. Their love enfolds you. When they pray, heaven acts. As they worship, spiritual climate changes. In their fight for right, the globe takes a turn for the better. Joy fills the house, peace covers it. Gentleness calms crisis and passion launches opportunity. How is your lover beautiful in spirit?

No Longer Dwarfed

Maggie's father was her best friend. A 22-year veteran of the Air Force, he decided to settle into civilian life and move his family to Florida. As they drove him to the train station so that he could prepare their new home, the car ran out of gas. Eleven-year old Maggie watched as her father left the car and began to walk into town to a service station.

After what seemed an eternal wait, a uniformed officer approached the car. He informed them that her father was dead, the victim of a massive heart attack. The last Maggie saw of her father was him walking away, his back to her, growing smaller into the horizon until, finally, he was gone.

Maggie became both inconsolable and uncontrollable. Over the next several years she immersed herself in drugs and promiscuity. By the age of 15 she became involved with a 27-year old man. By the age of 16 she gave birth to a baby boy. The father was abusive, and Maggie had no choice but to leave and try to support the child on her own.

In her attempt to survive, Maggie hooked up with another older man. He repeatedly beat her, threatened her family and forced her into prostitution to support their drug habit. One night, he brought home another woman. Maggie, upset, told him she wanted out.

He picked up a gun and said "You see that woman. In the morning I'm going to shoot her. Then I'm going to kill your boy. The last two bullets are for you and me."

Maggie believed him. As he slept, she picked up the gun, placed the barrel to his head and pulled the trigger. She phoned the police, informed them of what she had done, and asked them to take care of her son.

Though charged with first-degree murder, she was allowed to plead guilty to manslaughter. She received a five-year suspended sentence and three years of probation.

By her own admission, she left the courtroom as empty as when she entered. After all this, there was yet one more man, and one more threat to her life. This time she fled to her sister's place in North Carolina.

There she met Rich. Rich was a nice guy who treated Maggie and her son well. Rich's parents were followers of Jesus who practiced the Amish lifestyle. She and Rich couldn't have come from two different backgrounds.

Rich and Maggie married. The early part of their marriage was difficult. Within a year Rich moved out. A week later he gave her an ultimatum. Even though faith was not a big part of his life, he would move back only if she and her son would go to church. Only God could help the mess they were in. Despite her reservations, she agreed.

In the back pew of a little country church Maggie met love. She met it in the people that welcomed her there. She met it in the understanding of her in-laws. And she met it in Jesus: not a god who took away her dad, but the Savior who claimed her as his own.

Over time, Maggie and Rich learned what it meant to let go of fear and shame and to affirm the qualities and possibilities in the other.

Maggie and Rich later applied to Bible College, and despite only having a ninth grade education, Maggie was accepted. Five years later she graduated with a double degree, magna cum laude.

Untapped possibilities reside in you. The meaning of your life seeks to surface. You are not yet what you will fully be. Circumstances may have held you back but they do not tie you down. People may have underestimated you, but they cannot measure you. Inexperience may have charted your past but it doesn't determine your course.

You are more and more is in store.

Adam named his wife Eve ("living") because she would become the mother of all the living. Before this, she was referred to as woman. Adam named Eve after their failure in the garden. He named her after fear and shame distorted their relationship. Despite both of them aware of each other's shortcomings, Adam affirmed the meaning of Eve's life. Eve understood "God is not done with you." Eve knew she was more than the sum of her past and she knew more was in store.

You affirm the meaning of your partner's life. The beauty of your lover is not static. Their personal, social and spiritual life doesn't exist in a vacuum. Those qualities mean something to you and to people. Their absence affects you. Their presence brightens a day. Their influence matters. It has made a difference in you.

1. My wife believes with all her heart I am a writer whose words will help people. I doubt it often. I have grown up as a speaker. Writing has seemed beyond me. What do you see in your partner that still lies within?

2. I imagined certain things to be true of my life that have not come to pass. At my age, it's easy to let go. Has your mate given up on anything you still know will be true?

3. On my side of the family, it seems the women outlive the men. On my wife's side, it seems the men outlive the women. My wife and I don't like the thought of either going before the other. How about you? What will you miss about your partner? What can no one replace?

Love's First Kiss

How do I love you?
I need not count the ways.

For affirmation is not
In numbered calculation
But in the *pull of desire*
And in *waves of devotion.*

There's a great story about Samson, perhaps the most famous strong man of all time. He sees a woman and the text says "he talked to her and he liked her." I love that. It could have said anything: "He swept her off her feet or He picked her up." It could have read like a romance novel: "Samson's blue eyes pierced hers, his dark hair and square jaw framing his high forehead and straight nose. His sensuous mouth aglow with white teeth curved into a crooked smile. His powerful thighs anchored his enormous torso, his broad shoulders and ginormous chest eager to pull her to him." Nope. It says he liked her. I can imagine his buddies. "Hey big guy likes a girl." I bet he blushed.

I also like the story of Shechem. The text says "his heart was drawn to Dina and wanted her for his wife." He took her sexually before they married, and her family was furious. Shechem offered to pay any price they named to have her as his wife. Instead, they told him they could only give her to him if he and his tribe agreed to be circumcised. They agreed, and a little later in the story it says that after three days they were still in pain. Did I mention the pain? I mention it because when Shechem first heard the proposal, knowing full well knives shouldn't be cutting "down there," at his age, the text said "he lost no time in doing what they said."

Jacob was favored by his mom and was known for his smooth skin. Yet, he worked hard, manual labor for seven years in order to marry Rachel. The story says "they seemed like only a few days to him because of his love for her."

What is happening? A strong man has a boy-like crush. A grown man submits to a tricky procedure. A pampered boy works like a man.

Affirmation is expressed by desire.

Desire says "I'm drawn to you." Strong men open up new emotions. Noble men give up social norms. Gentlemen step up their wild side. The poet Holmes penned it this way:

I want you near at the first break of dawn when flowers are kissed by the dew.

I need your love like the earth needs the rain, like spring needs a heaven of blue.

I want your smile when the bright noonday sun caresses your cheek and your hair.

As you walk down the rose-bordered pathway, a picture of loveliness there.

I want to hear the sweet sound of your voice, to be with you wherever you are,

When God gently draws the curtains of night and fastens them shut with a star.

Solomon said:

- Be captivated by the love of your heart's desire.
- Rejoice in your lover always.
- Enjoy life with your partner for this is your reward.

To be captivated means to fill or to bathe. The idea is to be completely immersed in. To rejoice is to make glad or to brighten up. To enjoy is to see and behold.

How does your partner know you are immersed in them? *You connect with meaningful expressions.* The demonstration of your love means something to them. You have taken into account their likes and preferences, the small and big gestures that matter to them. You are aware that they are more practical or emotional or creative or intellectual and you tailor your expressions to suit their fit. You know if they prefer words or actions or touch or time or gifts or experiences. You exceed their daily dose of recommended affirmation.

How do you brighten your lover's life? *You communicate with heart-felt emotion.* Your sincerity massages their spirit. Your vulnerability opens their soul. Do you remember the glow of her face as you slid the ring on her finger? Do you remember the pride in his bearing as he sported his ring? Go there again. Go there more. Gifts with thought and heart behind them excite them. Acts that consider their need move them. Words spoken from a heart that listened enfolds them.

How do you enjoy life together? *You captivate with memorable experiences.* A simple twist on a normal activity becomes unforgettable. A plan built with shared anticipation reaches to new heights. A mystery the other awaits conceals the end but reveals loving motive; spontaneous turns the unexpected into the unparalleled.

In one survey of couples conducted by Dr. John Gottman, 80% said their marriages broke up because they gradually grew apart, lost the feeling of closeness and didn't feel loved and appreciated.

Emily Dickinson penned it this way:

> Crumbling is not an instant's act,
> A fundamental pause;
> Dilapidation's processes
> Are organized decays.
>
> Tis first a cobweb on the soul,
> A cuticle of dust,
> A borer in the axis,
> An elemental rust.
>
> Ruin is formal, devil's work,
> Consecutive and slow –
> Fail in an instant no man did,
> Slipping is crash's law.

Crumbling is arrested by being captivated with your lover.

One time my wife and I attended a conference at a retreat center. The number of people and the lack of rooms meant men and women had to sleep in separate quarters. By the end of the week I was done with that arrangement. Even though the event carried through the weekend, we made other arrangements for our Friday night stay. It wasn't glamorous. We were young parents on a thin budget. The economy hotel was surrounded by truck stops and serenaded by passing freeway traffic. But we were together.

The shower had room for one but the bed had room for two. My wife had barely dried off from the shower before I took her. My kisses were passionate, my embraces were furious and our finish was glorious. Nine months later our son was born.

Just like a man, some say. Absolutely. Like a strong man weakened by simple attraction. Like a noble man bowed to the majestic. Like a pampered man unleashed.

And my wife loved the meaningful expression of my leaving behind friends, bosses and responsibilities to be away and alone with her. She craved the primal heart-driven emotions she could see in my eyes, hear in my voice and feel in my body. She will never forget the time and place, the suddenness and fierceness or the husband I was in that moment. Desire conceived.

> One song, I have but one song, one song only for you/ One heart, tenderly beating, ever entreating, constant and true/ One love that has possessed me, one love thrilling me through/ One song my heart keeps singing, of one love only for you/ And away to his castle you'll go, to be happy forever we know/ Someday when spring is here, we'll find our love anew, and the birds will sing, and wedding bells will ring, someday when my dreams come true. (*Love's First Kiss*, Disney's Snow White)

I picture Samson humming the tune in-between his weight sets.

Heigh-ho

For years I thought the chorus of the Snow White song was "Heigh-ho, heigh-ho, it's off to work we go." I probably thought that because of the bumper sticker "I owe, I owe, so off to work I go."

But the chorus is actually "Its home from work I go."

In old Israeli law, if a master gave his servant a wife, the woman belonged to the master. When the time came where the servant could go free, he could leave but his wife had to stay. If the servant said, "I love my wife and do not want to go free" then the servant would have his ear pierced identifying him as the master's servant for life.

The same law also stated that if a man became engaged, he was to go home from military service so as to not die in battle. As well, if a man recently married, he was not to be sent to war or have any duty laid on him. For one year he was free to stay home and bring happiness to his wife.

Each of these laws honored the same value: *Affirmation is expressed by devotion.*

Home from work I go. I am devoted to you.

I would rather stay than leave. Our relationship comes before responsibilities; I enlisted for love, I'm drafted for war. What I must do I would rather not do unless I do it with you.

Devotion is presence. Presence demonstrates one's priority.

Presence isn't defined by occupying space. Presence manifests through *attention, awareness and active participation.*

Dr. John Gottman says "A romantic night out really turns up the heat only when a couple has kept the pilot light burning." Attention is the aphrodisiac of love. Turn toward the one you love to turn on the one you love.

One survey found that the happiest couples find fulfillment in the areas of communication, friendship, affection and sex more than in any other area such as lifestyle or financial stability. The most stress in a relationship for women relate to communication. The most stress for men iss the need for emotional connection. The common thread: attention.

Attention is devotion camped in your partner's world. You know their favorites, their wishes, their concerns, their memories, their safe places and the influences in their life.

Dr. Pat Love says that a couple "is not disconnected because they have poor communication; they have poor communication because they are disconnected."

Communication is attention to be given more than a skill to learn. Attention says to the partner, "I am here for you right now."

Awareness is devotion on alert. You are aware of what threatens your partner's sense of worth, belonging and confidence. You don't just listen to a rundown of the day's events or hear about who said what. You think about how incidents and remarks may be enemy agents in disguise, conspiring to upend your partner's confidence, connection and contributions. You ask "*How are you*" differently than others because you know your partner better than others. Awareness says, "I'm not only here for you, I will be there for you."

Active participation is devotion in action. One partner will do something *better* than the other or one will do something more *usually* than the other. Better and usually are not borders to keep out the other partner. Devotion lightens loads. Active participation says, "We share life not just space."

Jesus told a story about a farmer who planted seed. The worries of life, the deceitfulness of wealth and the desire for other things choked it out and made it unfruitful.

Affirmation is lost when distraction reigns, when distress consumes, when deceit dogs or misplaced desire leads astray. Their aim is the same: to remove one and keep one from home.

The beauty and meaning of my partner's life comes first. It comes before the career I excel in. It comes before the children we raise. It comes ahead of the dollars we bank and the closets we fill. It certainly is more important than anything we box and move. If I give more energy to strangers than to my marriage, the stuff of life will choke out the substance of life.

Jesus said "I am with you always." The message of his life is of God who is present: for you, with you, in you, living through you. You are his priority. So much so he left his home so that we could find our way home. His devotion flows from his desire. His prophet Zephaniah declared, "The

Lord your God is with you, the Mighty Warrior who saves. He will take great delight in you. He will rejoice over you with singing."

We love as he loves.

My Wife Sleeps With Prince Charming

Even though I sleep with 365 women a year, I try to make sure my wife sleeps with the same man.

He is the one who sees the best in her and wants the best for her. He is the one who celebrates her beauty and accentuates her worth. He is the one who is always drawn to her and does anything to be with her. He is the one who delights in her. Her laugh lifts him, her thoughts stimulate him, her character inspires him, her quirks amuse him and her body thrills him. He is the one who when absent wants nothing more than to be by her side, and when by her side imagines nothing that could compel him to leave.

He is the one who is not perfect. Sometimes he is anything but charming and far from being a prince. But he turns toward her. And he turns toward God.

She wakes to the beauty of all she is and he takes her hand and walks with her to Paradise.

> And away to his castle we'll go,
> To be happy forever we know
> Someday when spring is here,
> We'll find our love anew,
> And the birds will sing,
> And wedding bells will ring,
> Someday when our dreams come true.

The FUN Coach: Affirmation

How well do you see your partner? We can be a partner who acting out of our shame puts another to shame, or we can be a partner who in our nobility recognizes the nobility of the other.

1. How would you describe the beauty of your mate? What is best about them:

    - In body and mind. What physical qualities make you smile? What is it about the way they think or what they think that fascinates you?

    - In how they interact with others. What qualities do others see and admire?

    - In spirit. How do they influence the world around them?

2. Take the qualities above and put meaning to them. How has your partner's body and mind affected you positively? What is different today in your life because of these features? Describe those differences in *before and after* language. (Example: "Before I met my partner, I used to make decisions based on pros and cons. They have helped me to see more options and consider the larger picture.)"

3. Affirmation is expressed by desire.

    - You connect with meaningful expression. When was the last
      time your partner caught you by surprise in a pleasant way?
      What did they do and why did it mean so much to you? Name
      the longing that was validated or the fear that was alleviated.
      Now think about the last time you did that for you partner. Why
      did it mean so much to them – besides being thoughtful? What
      was at the heart of your expression?

    - You communicate with heart-felt emotion. Think about the
      words sincere, vulnerable and genuine. Picture a time you were
      communicating in these ways and your partner experienced that
      emotion from you. What was happening? Was it a look in your
      eye, a tone in your voice, a body posture? Was it word or action
      that made the difference? Ask your partner about this. How do
      they know you are trying to express deep emotion?

    - You captivate with memorable experiences. What was the last
      memorable experience that didn't cost much? Why was it
      memorable? List at least three reasons and then try for two
      more. What were the longings you were both fulfilling? What
      usual suspects of shame and fear was nowhere to be seen? Then
      think of a memorable experience that had cost to it. What was
      different between the two? What was not different as far as
      longings realized?

4. Desire is expressed by devotion.

    •   Attention camps in your partner's world. Let's do an elevator
        pitch about your partner. You are riding from the top floor to
        the lobby with no stops in-between. As the door closes, the
        person in the elevator says "Tell me about your partner." You
        may not talk about their job, family or personality. (By the way,
        let's pretend there is a hidden camera. You win money for every
        answer you give). Go!

    •   Awareness is alert to possible trouble. Your partner is telling
        you about their day. You are looking for things that may have
        affirmed or threatened their longings or tapped into their fears.
        Describe the last time you uncovered a threat before it could
        develop into a major issue. What triggered your alarm? Why
        were you so aware? Look back at the last time you didn't
        uncover a threat. What were the clues you missed? Now that
        you understand desires and fears, what are signs you might look
        for? Does your partner use certain words or phrases to signal
        concern? Do they exhibit the same emotions before tension
        explodes?

    •   Active participation shares life not just space. What is
        something your partner does consistently that can use a helping
        hand? What are things they are doing that can be taken off their
        plate? What are some areas you shared that have slipped over
        time?

- What keeps you away from home the most: worries of this life, deceitfulness of wealth or desire for other things?

The Toilet Paper Rolls Over The Top

Once I went on a four day hike into Glacier National Park. It was my first real hike. Until then, I considered walking the mall to be hiking enough. Whereas my wife loves walking, I love walking to the car.

My boss invited me. I was new on staff. He and a few other guys thought it would be a good opportunity to bond. I thought we could have bonded just as well at a ball game.

A four day hike meant three nights of camping. I don't like camping. I don't even like roughing it. Motel 6 is roughing it. Tents and sleeping bags are lack of progress.

I bought pre-packaged meals to take. They said gourmet on the label: so much for truth in advertising. I borrowed things I wouldn't use again, like hiking shoes. Did you know you can get blisters by walking in someone else's shoes? I wear a size eleven shoe. My blister was size twelve.

Giant flies live in Glacier Park. They sharpen their teeth on dead carcasses and then buzz around to sink those teeth in fresh meat. I must have been labeled gourmet. They ate better than I did.

Sure, the scenery was gorgeous. But so is my wife. And she was nowhere to be seen.

I bought what I couldn't stomach. I borrowed what didn't fit. I failed to protect myself against things that bugged me.

And I did it all to be accepted.

Have you ever not been yourself in order to be with someone else?

To be free means to be loved for who you are (affirmation) and as you are (acceptance). Acceptance understands that a person comes as is.

The word, accept, means to take to myself, to welcome or admit. Acceptance claims as one's own. Acceptance says "I can live with that." Nothing more is needed from you.

The message of acceptance is that you have nothing to prove and that you are not alone. You are welcome in. Let's make a home together.

I know I am not perfect. Some might call me slightly irregular. I can introduce you to people who exchanged me for a better fit. If a person does not accept me as is, then I might pretend to be what I am not, or withdraw to avoid rejection (and isolate myself to those like I am), or turn the fight onto them. No one wins when acceptance is lost.

Your partner is the single most important person you look to for acceptance. Neither of you will experience what it is to be truly yourself if acceptance is not freely exercised.

Dr. John Gottman is a professor of psychology at the University of Washington and cofounder of The Gottman Institute. He is a renowned specialist in marriage help. He writes:

Perhaps the biggest myth of all is that communication – and more specifically, learning to resolve your conflicts- is the royal road to romance and an enduring, happy marriage…After studying some 650 couples and tracking the fate of their marriages for up to fourteen years, we now understand that this approach to counseling doesn't work, not just because it's nearly impossible for most couples to do well, but more importantly because successful conflict resolution isn't what makes marriages succeed…The basis for coping effectively with either kind of problem is the same: communicating basic acceptance of your partner's personality. If either of you feel judged, misunderstood or rejected by the other, you will not be able to manage the problems in your marriage (*The Seven Principles For Making Marriage Work*).

Basic acceptance of your partner's personality includes their quirks and fears.

You have nothing to prove.

When my wife was recently in Italy for two months, I had to do laundry for the first time. Please don't hate me that I had never done laundry before. When you hear the rest of the story, you will understand why our washables have been protected from me. Neither the laundry nor I were happy with this development.

The big day came and I separated clothes by color and type of wash cycle. I had five monstrous piles. The first two loads were incident free. I started getting a little cocky, which is an *as is* quality of mine. I filled the washer for the third load. As I was doing dishes, I heard the washer kick in and realized I forgot to put in the detergent. I stopped the washer and added just the right amount. I was proud of myself for catching it because I would have hated to confess to my wife on Skype that I washed clothes without detergent. Later I finally finished the dishes and looked over at the laundry area. The third pile of clothes was still on the floor. I never put them in. I was washing water!

We all have quirks. I prefer to call mine charms. I think ten minutes early is on time. My books need to be organized by height and then color. My favorite cereal is chocolate.

My wife and I used to load the dishwasher in two different ways. Hers was the wrong way and mine was the right way.

Since I like things well-organized, it made sense to me to load the dishwasher by types: Bowls here, plates there and silverware sorted by spoons, forks and knives. Do it my way, and it is much easier and faster to unload.

Until my wife pointed out that my way didn't clean as well. Apparently, you have to mix it up to kill all the germs. My dislike for germs is greater than my love for organization. So I researched the subject. Turns out she is right.

Refusing to admit I am wrong is not one of my quirks. I just avoid it the same way I avoid spiders – another major quirk.

Research and surveys indicate that men regard their partners as their best friend. The majority of men do not want their wives to change in any significant way.

Quirks can be charming. Hillary Johnson writes that seductive men all possess a "flaw that punctuates perfection." With all my flaws, my perfection must be highly punctuated.

In her book *Swoon*, Betty Prioleau adds, "Pop psychologists and coaches who tout ironclad confidence as the key to sexual charisma may need a reality check. A hairline crack in a man's aplomb, a hint of vulnerability – either physical or psychological – can turn a woman inside out." Apparently that's why my wife looks different.

Erica Jong said "The things I find most appealing are their small imperfections."

Does your partner have quirks? There's a reason the guy is called Prince Charming.

Acceptance of quirks lays the foundation for greater trust. When you accept your partner for all their charms, you communicate several key messages:

- I don't need to change you.
- Different is not a threat.
- *As you are* is more attractive than *as they are*
- You can open up to me

Trust building is important because true acceptance goes beyond quirks. Our partners move in with baggage.

Behind every fear is desire. If I fear failure it is because I long for success. If I fear rumor it is because I want understanding. My fear of betrayal is a craving for commitment. I react to being ignored because I desire positive recognition. I want safety so I check under the bed for monsters.

When your partner moves in, they move in with positive desires and negative fears. The fear is rooted in shame, a false belief they cannot have what they desire because of who they are.

Affirmation answers their shame. It exposes the lie by applauding all that is true in your partner. Your affirmation smoothes the walls of shame: Fear has no foothold.

You are not alone

Marriage is a relationship unified by emotional attachment, emotional attunement and emotional attentiveness.
Attachment refers to a secure bond, a safe connection. In a secure relationship partners do not feel judged, misunderstood or rejected. Instead of negative thoughts simmering over time, partners view each other with

positive regard. When attachment is honored, partners are able to express their emotional need.

In her book, *Hold Me Tight*, Dr. Sue Johnson writes:

> Stepping aside from our usual ways of protecting ourselves and acknowledging our deepest needs can be hard, even painful. The reason for taking the risk is simple. If we don't learn to let our partner see our attachment needs in an open, authentic way, the chances of getting those needs met are miniscule.

Attunement means you are aware of your partner's emotions. You are not just aware of the surface emotion (she is angry) but the fear behind it (she is feeling shut out).

Attentiveness means you meet your partner's emotional need. Behind the emotion is a fear; the fear represents an unmet desire. Desire that is met alleviates the fear and vanquishes the shame.

Emotion is from the Latin word to move. Attachment moves toward each other; attunement moves in sync; attentiveness moves at the right pace. Picture the ballroom dance: together, in step, in rhythm.

Dr. Sue Johnson gives us two questions that facilitate attunement and attentiveness.

- What am I most afraid of?
- What do I need from you most?

The first question allows you and your partner to voice the pain and feelings you both are experiencing. The second questions voices what acceptance from each other would look like (I need to feel valued, close, respected, safe, etc.).

Fear has no foothold in the presence of affirmation. Footholds represent anything that promotes potential loss. Footholds take any form: criticism, rejection, failure, disappointment. Anything that acts against our deepest longings can be a foothold. Footholds come from multiple sources: family, friends, work and circumstance.

You gave them something - worth, companionship, understanding, honor, approval – and now it feels gone. Attentiveness is the opportunity to give it back: especially if you are the one who took it from them.

Forgiveness

"Forgiveness is the fragrance that the violet sheds on the heel that has crushed it (Mark Twain)."

When one partner is the source of the other's fear, the fabric of trust and emotional safety is torn. If acceptance says "you are in," injury is saying "get out."

Apology alone is not sufficient. Focus on what one did wrong does not give back what was lost.

Affirmation alone is not timely. If you tell me nine great things about me and one that is a real stinker, I leave thinking about the stinker.

The aim of forgiveness is restoration. Greeks defined the word restore as returning to an original condition. They used it in reference to mending a net or setting a bone.

There are four threads that knit trust and restore emotional attachment.

The first thread is compassion. This thread is knit by the offended partner.

Jesus taught to restore gently a person at fault. Gentle means strength under control. Sometimes people interpret forgiveness as an act of weakness.

Jesus says it is just the opposite. God is not weak when he forgives. It is the need to retaliate, to hold onto offense that is weakness.

Early Jewish Christians were told "Do not miss the grace of God and allow a bitter root to grow up and cause trouble."

Bitterness sets in when an offended person moves beyond the action of the injury and judges the intent and character of their partner. In the words of Dr. John Gottman, this leads to criticism and contempt. Whereas a complaint focuses on a behavior or specific action, criticism adds judgment. There is a difference between "I needed you to be home on time" and "You only think of yourself." Criticism leads to contempt, long-simmering negative thoughts in which bitterness takes root and disgust grows.

The second thread is confrontation. This is also sewn by the offended partner.

Confrontation recognizes that unless something is done the fabric of a relationship will remain torn.

The focus of confrontation is not on the guilt of the action. The focus is on the harm it has caused. Confrontation answers the question "What am I most afraid of?" The wounded partner is honest about their pain. They describe how their fear was given foothold. They name the action. That is a rightful complaint. The complaint is voiced without criticism.

As difficult as it is to probe the pain, it is better than the alternative. Typically, someone names an offense and the other person apologizes. The two of you are now supposed to act as if things are normal: an apology was offered and accepted. But what was lost has not been returned. Fear is not alleviated and emotional attachment is not secured. Soon, the offender will wonder why their partner cannot get over the injury. The goal of confrontation is healing and restoration, not guilt and remorse. Warm blankets of apology do not heal wounds that still bleed.

The third thread is confession. Confession is more than admission and apology. To confess is to say the same thing. It is to say the same thing as the person offended says about it. Confession acknowledges the pain because what your partner experienced is clear to you. You truly understand what was lost for them. You are emotionally attuned. You genuinely want them to have back what you took from them. The injured partner must see this in order to receive from you again.

The fourth thread is commitment to reconnect. Emotional attachment and attunement has been realized. You have moved toward each other and shared pain together. The attentive partner is now able to give what the offended partner needs most. What was lost is returned.

Growth is a marathon. Acceptance is the starting line. There are no false starts if truth is up front.

Marriage is the relationship in which we most become more. Samson told his dad, "Get her, she is the right one for me." The right one for you is the one who brings out the best in you.

Out of the Box

When my family has moved, most of our stuff is carefully wrapped and placed into boxes. These boxes get carried and stacked into a moving van, which if you think about it, is simply a box on wheels. When the door closes, I stand back, put my arm around my wife, and am reminded that everything we own is in a box.

Over the years, most moves required a larger box to move it. And generally, we moved to a bigger house, which is actually a box with doors and windows. We are now at the age where we have downsized, meaning our moving box and living box is smaller. But it is still a box.

Most days I leave my home box and go to the office box. I once had an office with an elevator. An elevator, of course, is a tight, confining small box, jam-packed with people suspended by cables you cannot see.

To get to the office I drive my car, which is a smaller box on cool wheels. As a boy, I even played with toy cars called Match*box*.

I help at church, which, unless careful, can become just another box, but with people and a steeple.

I have a friend named Jack who hides in his box.

Sometimes I try to think outside of the box. The problem is my thinking is done in a small box called the brain housed in another box called the head. I have a clever friend who, when told to think outside the box, responds, "What box?" Try telling that to the judge. Apparently some boxes come with bars. That's a box I prefer to think outside of.

 One day people will put me into a casket, which is a box without wheels. That should tell you something. They will put that box into a grave, which is a small opening into a very large box called Planet Earth.

This brings us to Jesus. Jesus is God who became man. People killed him and put him in a box. Jesus doesn't like it when people put him in a box. So he got out.

Don't you get tired of feeling boxed in? People try to wrap us up in their perceptions and expectations. Only the wrapping paper looks like all the same and the tags all read the same.

Lovers don't let their lover get boxed in. They rip off the tags, peel off the paper, open up the box and cherish the treasure they find inside.

Even if it comes *as is*.

The FUN Coach: Acceptance

1. You have nothing to prove! Just for fun, list some of your own quirks. Did anyone ever hurt your feelings over any of them? What has your partner done to assure you they are welcome home?

2. Consider some of the fears you identified earlier. What is the opposite desire you seek? Pick a word or phrase. (Example: If you fear looking bad, perhaps the opposite desire is admiration). Now do the same for your partner. What is the longing that is the flip-side of their fear?

3. You are not alone. What if anything blocks your ability to tell your partner what you fear most? Is the block with you or with your partner? Does attachment, attunement or attentiveness seem to be the biggest issue to resolve right now? Attachment means emotional safety is in place. Attunement describes awareness. Attentiveness moves to help.

4. Forgiveness can get pretty sloppy. It is rewarding but not easy. Which of the four dynamics seem most missing in your own experience of forgiveness: compassion, confrontation, confession or commitment to reconnect? If apology without real forgiveness has been your experience, what do the two of you need to add these dynamics into the mix? Do you need more teaching? A coach?

I'm On Your Side… Scoot Over

Rose Hartwick Thorpe writes of a soldier who was condemned to die by
execution at the ringing of a curfew bell. The soldier was engaged to be
married to a beautiful young girl named Bessie. As the sexton prepared to
pull the rope to ring the bell, Bessie climbed to the top of the belfry,
reached out and held on to the tongue of the huge bell at the risk of her life.
The sexton rang it and she was smashed against the sides of the bell but the
bell was silent. Once the bell ceased to swing, Bessie descended from the
tower. When General Cromwell approached, Bessie confessed:

> At his feet she told her story,
> Showed her hands all bruised and torn;
> And her sweet young face, still haggard
> With the anguish it had worn;
> Touched his heart with sudden pity,
> Lit his eyes with misty light:
> "Go, your lover lives," said Cromwell,
> "Curfew will not ring tonight."

> Wide they flung the massive portals,
> Led the prisoner forth to die
> All his bright young life before him,
> 'Neath the darkening English sky.

Bessie came, with flying footsteps,
Eyes aglow with love-light sweet;
Kneeling on the turf beside him,
Laid his pardon at his feet.
In his brave, strong arms he clasped her,
Kissed the face upturned and white
Whispered, Darling, you have saved me,
Curfew will not ring tonight."

We know what it is to await the ring of the curfew bell. A date has been set for layoffs. The hospital has scheduled the surgery. The divorce hearing is on the calendar. The in-laws arrive tomorrow.

Marriage was birthed out of need. Adam wasn't afraid of wild animal or tidal flood. No enemy shadowed him. No terror threatened to descend on him. He lived in paradise before there were governments, taxes and rents. But God looked upon him and saw the one need that rendered paradise futile. Adam was alone.

God is community: Father, Son and Spirit, three as one. For man to be made in God's image, man must be in community. Adam had no being like him with whom to relate. God arranged a marriage.

Need is not evil. Need is the pathway to greater fulfillment. Need is simply what is between here and a better there. Need exists to be met.

You need each other. You need the hug that holds you with assurance. Arms enfold you with familiarity. Your head finds its usual place against your partner's chest. Their soul wraps around your body, subtle changes in pressure signaling their support, strength and sensitivity. Peace and comfort flows over you as exotic oil.

Your lover needs your kiss. They need the moment your faces lean toward the other. They need the pause just before your lips meet, the pause that closes the shutters on what was and opens the door to what will be. As lips meet, they need the moist and gentle pressure with which it begins. Indicative of your love, they long for the moment when mouths open and the kiss becomes a rhythmic dance. Passion will push the kiss to frenzy; adoration will pull the kiss to the flow of a gentle tide.

Your heart needs the relief you feel when you return home and all the tasks that awaited you have been put to rest; you crave the ease of an evening home when your partner corrals the children and saddles them into bed on their own. No fire could replace the warmth of a blanket wrapped around you, a drink prepared for you and the conversation that follows.

You need lawns mowed and laundry folded, parents pacified and kiddos taxied. You need payments made and balances balanced. You needed it yesterday, need it now and need it before the weekend.

I've tried to hug myself and it's just not the same. I rub my own feet but the thrill is missing. As a kid I kissed my arm; I couldn't wait to grow up. Self-backrubs are impossible. I'd book a vacation for myself to an exotic island but who would I complain to? I figured out how to wash clothes, but I can't iron or make a bed wrinkle-free. I need.

My wife is short and can't reach everything and I'm happy to get it for her. I put the cap on too tight but I'm willing to undo it again. She doesn't enjoy finding greeting cards and I think of it as an exciting treasure hunt. She has physical needs only I can satisfy. I do.

The word advocate describes one called alongside to help.

Advocate was the word used to describe an ancient leader named Barnabas. He was originally named Joseph. I am rather fond of the name Joseph. My favorite verse in the Bible is Genesis 39:6 "Joseph was well-built and handsome." But Barnabas allowed his name to be changed. It means Son of Encouragement.

The same word for advocate is used of Jesus as Savior and the Holy Spirit as Counselor. We are never more an agent of God than when we advocate for our partner.

As an advocate, I assure my partner of three promises:

- I will choose and act with your best interest in mind.
- You can lean on me.
- We are in this together.

Everything I Do

Proverbs say a prudent wife comes from God. Prudent describes someone who has great insight and comprehension. She is contrasted with the quarrelsome and contentious wife. The contrast is in self-interest. Strife is a result of fighting for one's own wants. The insightful wife makes decisions with her husband's best interest at heart.

Husbands are told by God to flee sexual immorality and the pursuit of dishonest gain. The word fugitive derives from the word for flee. Men were to be on the run from actions that would harm their wives and family.

A decision and action is in your partner's best interest if it promotes their worth, belonging and competence. In other words:

- Does it meet my partner's deepest longings or does it give fear a foothold?

- Does this strengthen our emotional bond or weaken it? As a result of this choice or action, will my partner be inclined to move toward me or away from me?
- How does this affect my partner on the personal level? Does this accent their beauty? Does it align with their thinking? Does it promote their growth?
- How does this affect my partner socially? Does it further their good reputation? Does it cause them to feel awkward? Will they need to be secretive?
- How does this affect my partner spiritually? Does this negatively influence their positive influence? Does it cause them to feel closer to God or apart? Does it promote peace?

"Everything I do, I do it for you."

Eve took from the tree for herself but also gave to Adam. Abraham asked his wife to lie and say she was his sister so that a king would take her but not kill him. Compromise is not advocacy.

When Sarah planned to harm her servant, Abraham said "Do with her whatever you think best." He gave in. Conflict-avoidance is not advocacy.

Adam chose to treat Eve as a subordinate and ruled over her. Solomon said, "I find more bitter than death the woman who is a snare, whose heart is a trap and whose hands are chains." Control is not advocacy.

Your partner's best interest, even at personal cost and uncomfortable conflict is advocacy.

There's no love like your love
And no other, could give more love
There's nowhere, unless you're there…
You can't tell me it's not worth trying for
I can't help it, there's nothin' I want more
I would fight for you, I'd lie for you
Walk the wire for you, I'd die for you.
(*Everything I Do*)

Lean On Me

You are Adam or Eve. You once knew paradise. Now your insides feel torn apart, wrecked by guilt, sunk in shame. Where once you walked with God, now you are not sure where you stand.

You look across at your partner. Before, your naked bodies were a wonder to behold. Instead, foliage covers your differences. The leaves used to be green. Color seems to fade. The words wilt and crumble have become part of your vocabulary.

You hear footsteps. Last time you heard those steps, you hid. You realize there is no point. You wait and God approaches. He holds up garments of skin. He comes to you and wraps you in one. He doesn't drop it on you; he drapes you in it. He ensures its fit. "The climate has changed," he explains. "You will need it."

You look down and you see some stains. They couldn't be helped. Blood has spilled. It won't be the last time wrong is covered with blood.

That night, as you look at the stars and feel the hint of chill, you are warmed by more than a garment. You are warmed by grace. God, whom you turned from, turned to you. You can count on him.

Your name is Elkanah. You have two wives. You love them both and do what you can for them. One has born you children. The other cannot. Her name is Hannah. You see the undercurrent of sadness in her. She puts up a brave front, but the laughter of the children sings a mournful note. When she comes into your bed, you feel her hesitation. The pleasure of the shared bed was lost when her hope for children was dashed.

Each year you take your family to make sacrifice to God. It marks the year. The wife who bears your children sees it as a holiday. She builds the children's excitement. The barren one looks upon the sojourn as an annual reminder of what she is not. She will seek God again. Perhaps this year her entreaty will be answered.

At the feast, you give Hannah a double portion of meat. You love her. You want her to be happy. She smiles; the gesture is kind. The invitation is sincere: lean on me. For some things, she will. For a child, she will lean on God alone. You hope he answers too.

Bill Withers sings "Lean on me when you're not strong, and I'll be your friend, I'll help you carry on; for it won't be long 'til I'm gonna need somebody to lean on."

Old Israel law declared if a man married another woman, he must not deprive the first one of food, clothing and sex (I would like to have listened in on his conversation with the second wife: "Gee, honey, rules are rules"). The word for deprive means to keep back, reduce or cut short.

Followers of Jesus were taught, "If anyone does not provide for his family he has denied the faith and is worse than an unbeliever."

Lack of provision denies faith? Faith doesn't just mean you believe in God. Faith means you partner with God. You say yes to what he wants to do through you for others. And home is always the first place God begins.

Fail to provide and I am worse than an unbeliever? An unbeliever doesn't describe someone who just thinks wrongly about God. It describes the person who acts against God. Believe God but fail to provide and you work against God.

Husbands and wives were told, "Do not deprive each other sexually."

We feel secure with our lover when we know we can reach out and they will be there for us. The partner who provides closeness, understanding and support – emotional, material and physical – reinforces their love and our sense of worth, belonging and competence.

When our partner holds back what we need, unease arises. It's not so much about a need being unmet. The issue is they choose to limit who they are to us. They are no longer our advocate. We become anxious not at what's missing in our life but at what might be lost in our relationship. We hear the toll of a curfew bell. And we feel very much alone.

Nothing's Gonna Stop Us Now

After the dust settled, "Adam lay with his wife Eve."

You are David or Bathsheba. Books have been written and movies made of your first sexual encounter. It is sewn into history with a scarlet letter. Recriminations have resounded; judgments have been pronounced. You are the main meal of moralizing ministers and the preferred passage of pulpit pounders.

Few write or tell of the pain of your heart. Barely a word is spoken at the loss of the child you carried. You mourned.

No pen tells of what happened next. Ministers are mute on the message. Teachers are timid with the text.

David finds his wife. Not the adulteress. Not the woman of a one-night stand who bore the reminder of their folly. Her face is still stained with tears. Her eyes red, they are a startling contrast to the life he once saw in them. Her hair that once glowed in the light of the moon is unwashed and unkempt. She is wrapped and blanketed and still cold.

He places his arms around her and holds her to him. His fingers reach for her hair and pull the strands from her face. He kisses her forehead and looks into her eyes. She looks back. She sees not the lust of a man. Nor does she see the authority of a king. She sees tender love. One gaze, one hold, and her heart is touched with life.

They do not speak as he lays her down. Little is said as he pulls himself under her cover. Clothes are not removed, just rearranged. He enters. She receives.

Adam lays with Eve; David with Bathsheba. Are they just sex-starved men?

Or are they two men with the same message for their wives: We are in this together.

Eve would become the mother of all the living just as God had promised. Bathsheba would give birth to a child in the royal line and her name would be recorded in the genealogy of Jesus the Savior.

> Looking in your eyes I see a paradise
> This world that I found is too good to be true.
> Standing here beside you
> Want so much to give you
> This love in my heart that I'm feeling for you.
> Let em say we're crazy
> I don't care about that
> Put your hand in my hand, baby
> Don't ever look back.
> Let the world around us just fall apart
> Baby we can make it if we're heart to heart

And we can build this dream together
Standing strong forever
Nothing's gonna stop us now.
And if this world runs out of lovers
We'll still have each other...
Whatever it takes I will stay here with you
Take it to the good times
See it through the bad times
Whatever it takes is what I'm gonna do.
(Diane Warren and Albert Hammond lyrics: Nothing's Gonna Stop Us
Now performed by Starship)

November 20, 1937. Frankie knew he was in trouble. The brakes on the coal car were failing, and it would only be moments before it crashed into the coal car ahead. Two men, unaware of the runaway car, were cleaning out the remains of the coal from the last load. Death was imminent.

Frankie jumped from the runaway car and raced ahead warning his friends. As impact neared, he jumped back into his coal car and gave a last desperate yank on the brake wheel. The brakes were unresponsive, and the car crashed into the other. Frankie was hurled forward and out the left side of the car. He grabbed for a hold with his right arm and the left side of his body slid under the wheels, severing his left leg immediately and crushing his left arm between the wheel and the track.

Frankie would be in and out of the hospital over the next six months. His left leg was missing, and his left arm was gone from below his elbow. He learned to walk with the aid of a crutch. His wife, Margaret, says he never complained about his condition. He was later awarded the Carnegie Medal for the heroism he displayed in saving the lives of his friends.

One day, years later and after Frankie had passed away, his wife was talking to her grandchildren about their grandfather. They were asking questions about how he would get around, how we would garden and work.

"Oh, he just seemed to do it," she answered.

"The hardest thing," she continued, "Was when he carpentered. I'd have to hold the nails for him, and he'd swing the hammer." Margaret held nails while her one-armed, one-legged husband swung a framing hammer at both the nail and her fingers.

Frankie was a hero. He saved the lives of two men. So was Margaret. She held the nail.

The FUN Coach: Advocacy

Marriage was birthed out of need. Advocates help.

1. An advocate chooses and acts for the best interest of another. When was the last time you made a decision or did something that reflected your own self-interest? What were you trying to satisfy? Why did you do it even if it was against your own partner's interest? Has your answer uncovered an aspect of shame or fear that motivates you? Let's turn the table: Your partner acted in their interest but not yours? First, do you see what motivated them? Second, describe your emotion. Now let's be positive: What is an upcoming decision or opportunity you have to act in your partner's best interest?

2. Define the last three times you were able to provide what your partner needed. How did it feel knowing they could lean on you and you delivered? What part of your deepest longing was met? When is the last time you deprived your partner or felt deprived by them? What was happening beneath the surface of events? If you didn't give at the time, why? What was the immediate reason but what was also the internal reason? When you last felt deprived, what did you need – not the material need but the internal need?

3. What did your partner do recently to communicate to you "we are in this together?" Is there a current situation that calls for an "in it together" gesture?

Every Marriage Should Be
A Nudist Colony

A young woman walks along the fence line. Her hair is long, untied. A simple white shirt hangs over faded jeans. The sun casts its glow upon her, too early in the afternoon for it to beat on her, enough past morning that the air is no longer tinged cool.

As she walks, her hand glides lightly over each picket in the fence. Her gaze seems focused but not present, thoughts elsewhere. She steps casually, unhurried. Her hips sway like hung sheets moved by a gentle breeze, her shoulders rise more than bounce.

Her mouth lifts in smile every few steps.

She recalls the words of the poet. Too amazing is the way of a man with a woman. She ponders the word *way*. Poets employed it to picture a road and an exchange. A road, much like the one she was on: open, walked by many yet each course different, no origin or destination the same. An exchange, words traded back and forth until the meaning one intends is received by the other. An act of one met in kind, rhythm experienced by two.

Her memory returns to last night. Side by side they sat. She snuggled into him as he kept his arm around her. His strong hand was gentle with caress

but firm when it squeezed. That one simple act the sum of all she loved about him. She found safety in his strength and sensitivity.
Her words had been many but his attention was constant. Before the evening ended, he grabbed her glass and refreshed it with water. That, too, touched her heart. The extra effort he showed in dating didn't end after their wedding. Marriage seemed to intensify the meaning of the simplest act of love.

She came to her favorite spot in the road. If she continued straight she would lose the fence line; a simple right turn and she would walk between a grove of trees on her left and the field opposite. She chose the road between.

Hands in pocket, she slowed her step ever slightly. The word *unfolding* came to mind. She knew the field next to her better than any. As a girl she played in its grass until the stains in her clothes became a permanent part of their color scheme. She lifted flowers to her nose, pretending they were a gift from her long awaited prince. Her favorite dog chased whatever she threw. His simple grave was still marked by the cross she made from sticks he returned to her. The trees beside her were dense. Changes of seasons seemed also to change the nature of their grove. Her exploration never seemed complete. The trees seemed the same but their stance different. Sudden growth, changes of color, weathered endurance, spring's renewal: she marveled at the magic of seeing clearly but never seeing fully.

She remembered fondly how tears filled her husband's eyes the night before their daughter started school. He was sensing loss, she was feeling accomplishment. One experience marked with different emotions made the whole experience seem more complete. She had kissed him with lingering assurance that night. Her own dreams seemed sweeter.

Does life change or do seasons change? What unfolds, reveals.

She freed her hands from her pockets and swung her arms freely. Her pace didn't really quicken so much as move to a beat. Her steps had jazz in them.

How had he done that? She let her senses re-engage that night. Three weeks ago now, it still seemed like yesterday. He took her into the city. Their table overlooked the river, the glow of light-posts lining the walkway reflected off the water. The center candle burned steadily, accenting his facial features with shades of mystery and revelation. She could lose herself in those deep, green eyes. She smiled to herself. She did lose herself in those eyes. Over the table, her eyes settled on his lips and she felt her hunger grow. Elegant linen hosted their setting; fine cloth was opened to reveal their ware.

He led her to a guestroom he had reserved in advance. They stepped into each other's arms and then stepped together in orchestrated dance. Their garments flowed to the floor like feathers are eased down by the wind. Limbs entwined, lips embraced and two became one. She remembered the scent of his skin, the spark in his eyes and the stillness of his breath in the aftermath of its rush.

Two as one. She stopped at her favorite log. Sitting down, she picked at a dandelion that hugged a fence post. Mom and dad divorced when she was young. She found out later he had an affair. She thought a lot about that before her own marriage. It could happen to anyone. she looked for the signs before they married.

"You're looking for the wrong signs," her friend said.
"What do you mean?"

"You are looking to see if he notices other women. Of course he notices. Beauty compels looks. You know that."

"Then what do I look for?"

"You need to look for two things," her friend said. "The first is if he treats women as a commodity. Think about it. It's hard enough being married to one person. Why would any guy marry two? Yet, multiple marriage is as old as time. Are you telling me a guy poured himself so selflessly into love for his wife that he thought it would be great to multiply his efforts with another wife, or three or four? Multiple marriage wasn't about the guy giving it was about the guy getting. Are you following me?"

"That makes sense."

"Now, add to that the fact that some of those guys not only had wives, they had concubines. So now they are compartmentalizing their women: one for children and chores, the other for sex. Then they hire prostitutes. Variety, I guess. But that's what I mean. Women as commodity, as a good; as in, are you good for me?"

"So the question to ask yourself is: Does this guy you love treat other women selflessly? Does he talk about women respectfully? Not just women, really. Is there any sign he classifies people in terms of what they can do for him?"

She thought about the time she went shopping with her father. They were helped by a clerk who was much younger than he. She heard him tell her, "If only I were younger." Until now she would have assumed he was being complimentary or playful. She didn't realize there was a deeper issue. How her father saw people.

"Ok. What's the second sign?"

"How does he allow himself to be treated?"

"What are you saying?"

"There's a proverb that says a prostitute reduces a man to a loaf of bread. It's reverse commodity. He lets himself be treated indignantly. Everyone always looks at the prostitute as the one cheapening her value. But who walks away with the money? "

"I never saw it that way before."

"It is an act of reduction not seduction. So how does this man of yours guard his dignity?"

"Look honey. People worry about the wrong thing. Your man likes sex? I hope so. Does he find other women attractive? Let him be honest about it. I crushed on the new barista in town. Big deal. Just because he makes my day feel like a Grande doesn't mean I'm swapping sugar packs with him. It's not a matter of your man's intention or his ability to make a commitment or his Dudley-do-right nature. How does he see people and how does he see himself? Does he prey or is he prey? Both are bad news."

She got up from the log and continued walking. She considered how two as one is sexual and spiritual. Knit together. She breathed him in. Not the scent of his body in their act of love but his spirit that filled her own. How is it possible, she wondered, that his emotions can lift hers? How does just being with him change her perspective, break her negative thoughts? She knows she does the same for him.

She approaches her favorite tree. It looks like two at a distance until you get close. One base but two trunks rise up, their branches woven together. She thinks not only of how two are one but of how one is more than two; how she and her husband are so much more than if they were apart. Love doesn't add up. Maybe it's not supposed to be reduced to mathematical equation or scientific precision. There is a mystery to marriage she only wants to probe but never really solve.

Marriage At The OK Corral

The cop busted us.

When my wife and I were dating in high school, we parked the car one night in a secluded area. I'm not sure if it was the steamy windows or the brake lights flashing like morse code that caught the officer's attention. All I know is there was a knock on the window, a flashlight in my face and red and blue lights in my rear view mirror. I rolled down the window.

"Miss, are you okay?"

He could have said so many things:

- "What are you doing?" (Rhetorical question, obvious answer)
- "What were you thinking?" (Rhetorical question, obvious answer)
- "Girl, couldn't you have done better than him?" (Rhetorical question, obvious....)

The police officer could have said anything, but he asked one thing: Are you okay?

My wife said, "Yes, I am okay."

When a light is shown on our life and focused on what should not be, we expect to be judged. Instead, God asks if we are okay.

God wants each person in marriage to be free and to be united. Marriage has an element of mystery. Two become one and yet one is more than two. Somehow not only do two bodies unite but two spirits are knit. A couple is not only seen as together, they are quite actually together.

The very essence of marriage is two people who join in relationship to benefit the other. Selfish makes two. Selfless makes one.

Marriage is not just mystery it's mutuality. We are God's way of making sure the other is okay. Though we may be different in many ways, we are for each other.

How Do You Walk In Those Shoes?

Does research ever frustrate you? It seems you read one thing and a little while later a different report questions the findings of the first. Maybe that's why they call it re-search.
We (and by that I mean not me) are still discovering the differences between men and women and how their brains are wired and how certain regions differ in size and why therefore men are more this and women are more that. We (and by that I do mean me) don't fully know.

Supposedly, women ruminate over emotions, negative feelings and negative memories more than men. Women remember more details and their narratives are longer. This is apparent evidently by age three. Women prefer stories. Men prefer highlights.

Part of the deal is that women are more efficient at processing both sides of their brain, the emotional and the logical, at the same time. Men tend to use one side at a time. No, men don't have half a brain. They are only using half at a time. It's energy efficiency. This is also why men compartmentalize more than women.

Men like to think of marriage as a place to relax. Women gain security from interaction. However, talking that becomes intimate causes a higher physiological arousal in men than it does women. If a man feels something, he has to do something. So, ladies, talk all you like. Just watch what you talk about.

Women are more discriminate. In her book *Forty Beads*, Carolyn Evans writes:

"When we see a hot guy, the first thing we might do is start sizing him up as far as how he might fit into our life. Sure, he's hot, but I wonder what he does? Where is he from? Are those no-iron slacks? Eww! It can be something as minor as a polyester blend (well, that's not really so minor) that will cause us to kick him to the curb even before we exchanged sugar packets at the Starbucks counter."

Or to put it another way: There is a book called *1001 Questions To Ask Before Marriage*. That had to be written for women. Men have two questions. One before and one after: Will you marry me? How is tonight looking?

Many differences are not gender based. They are personality based; quirks and fears. It's hard to blame my love for country music on being male. My wife thinks it's a quirk and her fear is I will play it when we are in the car.

Wiring is one thing. Wounds are another.

Most needs are not gender based. Male and female have the same essential needs because they are human. I've seen rankings of supposed differences between men's needs vs. women's needs. After reading them, I turned to my wife and said, "I might be a woman."

Our needs (which are the same by nature) differ only in importance, extent and how they are met (which varies by nurture).

My wife and I are wired to meet needs differently. But we meet the same needs.

Paige Anderson Swiney writes of the time she was in a hurry in the commissary. In the soap aisle, an aged man stood in her way. She noticed a tear in his eye as he stared at the soap. She asked if she could help, and he told her he was looking for his wife's brand of soap. She offered him her phone so that he could call her.

"She died a year ago," he said. "I just want to smell her again."

You know what it is to so love another their very absence leaves a void only they can fill. You've looked forward to trips even though it meant being away from your partner. Then, once away, your heart felt empty. The need to get away, the relief of interrupted routine pales against the reality of love's separation. When my wife was away in Italy, I would climb into bed, pull her photo next to me and keep hitting my phone's backlight until sleep finally took me.

The void is great because we allow our partner to fill us. We receive everything they have to offer. It doesn't matter that they are different. It matters that we draw from them.

And that is the meaning of the word submission.

Jesus taught husbands and wives to submit to each other. People have managed to ransack the definition and exploit its meaning. They use the definition "line up under" to describe one who obeys authority. The key to understanding the meaning of submit is in its association with the word head (as in husbands are the head of their wives). The word head wasn't only used to describe authority. It was used to describe the source or origin of something. You have to compare the two definitions in order to determine the meaning. Both authority and source have one common trait: something worthwhile to offer. Submit means to receive fully.

So when a husband says to me "My wife won't submit" I ask "What do you have worth offering?"

Multiple studies show that the number one source of happiness and satisfaction for a couple in marriage is their friendship; more so than sex, children, health, career or finance. The emotional bond and positive regard they have with each other helps them navigate the rougher waters and negativity that comes into any relationship. They fill each other up.

That's why the number one quality men want more of in marriage is communication. The second is affection. It's why two-thirds of men and women want more romance in their marriage. Neglect kills love. Lack of togetherness means greater inability to cope with pain. Bonding promotes physical and emotional well-being.

The type of communication couples desire leads to greater emotional attachment.

Listening is attuned to emotions and speaking is attentive to emotions.

Proverb says one who speaks before listening is a fool. Couples who are for each other, who look to see if the other is okay, employ three priorities in listening:

1. Listen for the emotion behind the words.

Emotions reveal well-being or fear. Words that are positive, joyful or peaceful convey a person in touch with their deepest longings. This is the time to celebrate. Proverb says "Let another praise you."

Words that are negative, confused, frustrated or angry reveal possible footholds of fear. Your partner's sense of shame is heightened. You have opportunity to clarify if this is true and offer comfort: "What do you need most from me right now?"

2. Listen to understand the words.

People have different beliefs, interpretations and expectations. The conflict you are experiencing may be due to a difference in perception.

A belief may be true or false. A partner may believe that silence is a sign of something wrong in the relationship. The other partner believes silence is a sign of security in the relationship. A person may ask, "Why are you mad at me?" believing your silence is a bad thing and interpreting it differently than you intended.

An interpretation is the lens through which we judge words, actions and events. They are usually tied into our fears. You may not understand why your partner is so angry at your friend. They laughed when your partner made an honest mistake. You thought it was funny too. Your partner was offended. They interpreted laughter through their fear of looking bad. You interpreted the laughter as unconditional acceptance from a friend.

If later that evening you defend the friend, you will have missed the point. Your partner has a fear foothold that needs to be removed by your clarification and comfort.

An expectation is a pre-determined outlook. Expectations are usually tied into our shame. Your partner believes conflict is bad. They interpret conflict as a sign of disapproval and a step toward distance. They expect that if two people experience conflict, one will leave. You believe conflict is good. You interpret conflict as a desire to be close and an attempt to remove barriers. You expect conflict to make a relationship better and draw two people closer.

   3.   Listen for the next best question.

Questions are your friends, allies and advocates. Used wisely, they draw out your partner's thoughts and emotions. You are able to validate them. Asking "What's wrong?" and then hearing about the problem is not listening. Listening asks the questions that draw out the true fear and reveal the best way to meet their need.

Love is listening. Listening makes your partner the sole focus of your interest. One woman contrasted a disastrous date with a dream date. Of the first, she said, "When it was over, I knew everything about him and he knew nothing about me."

The aim of listening is conversation. Women in polls complain about men's inability to engage and interest them. Silence is their number one complaint. It's not the content that matters but the attachment, attunement and attentiveness. Conversation promotes companionship and connection.

Sometimes communication gets rocky.

My wife and I once had a raccoon problem. The female raccoon chose to camp on our wood-shingled roof. Then she decided inside would be better. It had something to do with wanting to nest in our house. We did not accept her. That was unacceptable to the raccoon. So she began to dig through our roof.

One day I was out of town. My wife had enough with the raccoon. She tried reasoning, but one doesn't reason with a nesting mother. The girl fight was on. As the raccoon stared down from the roof, my wife calculated distance and velocity. The raccoon didn't see the rock coming. She didn't see the rock coming because it never made it there. My wife is petite. I'd say she throws like a girl but that would be giving her too much credit. She did hit the living room window though. When I got home, I laughed and made two phone calls: one to the glass company, the other to a trapper.

Have you ever had rocks thrown into your communication?

Remember all those conflict-resolution techniques you are supposed to employ? I didn't think so. And it doesn't matter, because as we quoted earlier they aren't the secret. Most couples just don't do that stuff well. So how do you repair the break?

    1.   Your partner hears two voices. Make yours stand out.

Every fear has a voice associated with it. It could be the controlling voice of a father, the critical voice of a mother, the contentious voice of a sibling or the condemning voice of a teacher or coach. We all grow up with voices.

Just as certain scents can trigger a memory, certain issues hit the play button of recorded voices. You may be talking but it's not your voice they hear.

Your voice becomes dominant when you stay focused on alleviating fear and promoting longing. The way you listen and the way you apply the next two insights pauses their inner critic.

    2.   Start well to end well.

A good start begins with complaint (focus on the issue) not with criticism (blame and fault). "We have a problem" not "You are the problem." The problem is clearly explained and offered with respect for the other.

A good start expresses what the person is feeling. As much as a person can identify the fear and shame at stake, they bring it out into the open.

The problem is associated with a desired outcome. What is the well-being the couple wants to experience? What is the shame and fear partners want to avoid giving foothold to?

A good start focuses on one issue at a time. It doesn't bring up the past and overload the present.

The key to a good start is patience.

3.   Move toward shared solution not cease-fire.

"We agree to disagree" leaves the chords of emotional attachment dangling. The presenting issue isn't the problem. The fear foothold is the problem. The surfacing of shame is the issue. Your relationship is on the slide because someone's fear wants to address a problem and someone's shame wants to avoid acknowledging the problem.

Cease-fire is not peace.

Repair is accomplished when both partners can lead the conversation to the place where each can admit:

- What am I most afraid of?
- What do I need most from you?

Couples identify lack of communication skill as their big problem. It isn't.

You love your partner. You looked to the time you would have every day together. You affirm who they are and accept their quirks and fears. You are their advocate. What you say communicates your love or not. That's the issue. Build up and help. Or diminish, tear down and break hearts. You know what your partner finds funny or helpful and you know what they find painful (and feelings literally get hurt). You know because you once said something that backfired. You apologized and were given another chance. Why the repeat offense? It is impossible to speak before you think. Communication isn't about skill, it's about spirit. You did not marry to hurt the person. You married to help. That's what communication is all about.

When it comes to harmful communication, you have to trap the culprit together. Then you can see your way clear again.

Not Okay

Jesus said "Love your neighbor as yourself." His followers taught "Love does no harm to your neighbor." They added, "Husbands, love your wives as Christ loved the church and gave himself up for her…Husbands should love their wives as their own bodies. He who loves his wife loves himself."

Mutuality watches out for the other. Jesus made the concept easy to understand: the same way you watch out for your body and love your body, watch out for your partner.

I am acutely aware of what might harm my body and I protect against those things. I avoid killer bees, poisonous spiders and Burger King.

I am willing for my body to feel pain. I lift weights, firm my glutes and cut my hair.

Therein is the difference. I don't like pain. However, a difficult conversation in which I realize painful realities can lead to greater strength in relationship. It hurt but it hurt so good. Harm is not good.

Anything that promotes shame and fear and minimizes worth, belonging and competence is harmful. There are several usual suspects.

Blame poisons affirmation.

One bite is all it takes and beauty is lost. In every marriage, needs must be expressed. But there is a big difference between voicing need and assigning failure.

At the heart of blame is avoidance of our shame. Blame rots affirmation by creating distance and defensiveness. When I blame my partner, I take a step back. Rather than turning toward, I have turned from. Each thought of blame, whether spoken or not, is another step in the wrong direction. When my partner feels blame, and they will feel it even if they do not hear it, they raise a shield is to protect their worth. The mirror they look into is reflecting distorted images. They will withdraw so as to look away or they will crack the mirror in frustration.

"Much of the resentment that occurs in relationships is not about material unfairness; it's about the perception that your emotions are controlled, if not manipulated, by your partner – he makes you anxious, and she makes you feel like a failure (Dr. Patricia Love, *how to improve your marriage without talking about it*)."

Have you ever wondered if things could have been different for Adam and Eve? They ate from the tree of the knowledge of good and evil. When God asked why, Adam blamed "the woman you gave me." Eve blamed the devil. Neither one apologized. Neither one admitted their failure. Neither one turned toward God or the other. Neither one voiced fear or need. They digested the evil of non-disclosure.

Life went on. They knew of God but did not live with him. It would be several generations until their children "began to call on the name of the Lord." Adam and Eve lived together and had kids, but they didn't experience being free, being united or being made new. She felt subordinate. He felt separate.

What if they had turned toward God and toward each other? What would have happened if they brought their fear and shame into the open? As far as eternity, nothing would have changed. God would have come in the person of Christ to take away the evil that had been digested, to reconcile people to God and to each other and to take us home with him. But maybe the family system that led to Cain killing Abel and men marrying multiple wives and nations at war with each other and inequality expanding - maybe that could have been different.

We think of Adam and Eve's great sin as the one act of disobedience in which they ate from the tree. But which became the greater issue: Their failure or their response to failure?

The mirror of acceptance is shattered by the rocks of comparison and competition.

Jacob worked for seven years in order to marry Laban's daughter Rachel. Rachel is described as lovely in form and beautiful. She had an older sister named Leah, who was described as having weak eyes.

The wedding day came and the next morning Jacob woke up to find that he had married Leah (I don't know how that could happen either. I suspect veils and drink). Anyway, Jacob complained, so Laban gave him Rachel as well.

Jacob loved Rachel more than Leah.

The tale of two sisters played on, the plot twisting in the winds of comparison and competition. Rachel was barren and unable to give Jacob children. Leah became pregnant easily and frequently.

In giving Jacob children, Leah thought, "Surely my husband will love me now."

Rachel became jealous of her sister. She said to Jacob, "Give me children or I'll die!" He said, "Am I in the place of God?" That was a nice Hebrew way of saying, "What are you looking at me for?"

Eventually, God enabled Rachel to give birth to a boy she named Joseph (later described as well-built and handsome).

Leah paled in comparison to Rachel. Rachel came up short in competing against Leah.

Both felt the blow of shattered acceptance.

Comparison and competition work the opposite effect of acceptance. Instead of having nothing to prove, you have everything to prove. Instead of knowing you are not alone, the one person you need the most is weighing out your differences and suspending judgment about your worth.

You feel at risk. Risk fuels fear. Fear feeds shame. You will withdraw or you will attack.

Comparison and competition plays out in the arenas of the personal, social and spiritual. Those are the areas in which your beauty flourished and the meaning of your life was clear. Now, what you once had confidence in threatens your well-being. What makes you – you - may not be good enough.

"Mirror, mirror," we ask. "Who is fairest? "Not you," we hear.

Or do we? At times it seems the standards are unclear. We are unsure what we hear our mirror saying. It's hard to win when your partner holds the subjective score of the match.

That's why acceptance is so awesome. Acceptance gives the score in advance. "You win. You have home field advantage. I compare all to you not you to them. Whatever is lost I return. It's a given." Acceptance alleviates the fear that comparison and competition stir.

Advocacy feels opposed when our partner is lined up on the other side.

The proverb says a quarrelsome wife is like a constant dripping on a rainy day. The story of Samson, the strong man, says he was tired to death from his wife's nagging.

Hannah wept over her inability to bear children. Her husband said to her, "Why are you weeping? Do I not mean more to you than ten sons?'

Israeli law prescribed what a man was to do if feelings of jealousy came over him?

Quarreling and nagging; insecurity and self-centeredness; jealousy. It makes you want to ask, "What are you doing over there? I thought you were on my side."

Disagreements and complaints happen. They can be healthy if they bring needed correction to the relationship. They prevent harm. Quarreling and nagging give it a different shade: blame and shame. Complaint (I need) turns to criticism (you failed). Criticism turns to contempt. Affirmation, acceptance and advocacy are long gone. Criticism and contempt drain you until one day you are done fighting (tired to death of the relationship).

Insecurity is subtle opposition. Your partner stands near but makes you feel like you are moving away. "Do I not mean more to you?" Elkanah asked. He was aware of his wife's emotions (she is downhearted) but he was not attuned (her physical barrenness has harmed her spirit).

Jealousy is misunderstood. It's a neutral emotion, meaning it can be good or bad. When God says "I am jealous for you" he isn't expressing insecurity or fear. He knows what is best for you, and he fights for your best interest. But jealousy rooted in insecurity is driven by self-interest. Your jealous partner is focused on what they might lose. False jealousy is concerned about being harmed; true jealousy is concerned with your partner being harmed.

God intended sex to unite two. Satan intends sex to divide all.

Sex divides when we allow the words of another to satisfy unmet emotional needs in our marriage. Proverbs remind us: "For the lips of an adulteress drip honey, and her speech is smoother than oil." "Keep from the smooth tongue of the wayward wife." "With persuasive words she led him astray; she seduced him with her smooth talk."

Sex divides when we indulge without thought to consequence. "Why embrace the breasts of another man's wife." "I find more bitter than death the woman who is a snare, whose heart is a trap and whose hands are chains." "I denied myself nothing my eyes desired; I refused my heart no pleasure. Everything was meaningless, a chasing after wind."

I'm Okay, You're Okay

The core quality of mutuality is the helper you are to the other. Again, helper refers to divine agency. Helper is not something anyone can do. Helper is what you are placed to be for this person. God is using you, not another, to come alongside your partner. God has words and actions he intends only for you to speak and do.

God shines his light on your marriage. He has one question: Are you okay?

The movie *Saving Private Ryan* opens with the Allied invasion of Normandy in World War II. Two brothers are killed in the action. A third brother had been recently killed in a different conflict. Their mother was scheduled to receive all three telegrams on the same day notifying her of their deaths. An Army Chief of Staff learns that a fourth son, Private James Ryan, is missing and possibly still alive. He sends Captain Miller and seven other soldiers who had survived the Normandy invasion to find him.

In the movie, a number of the soldiers wonder at the rationale of risking eight lives for one. Captain Miller says the following:

> "Sometimes I wonder if I've changed so much, my wife is even gonna recognize me whenever it is I get back to her, and how I'll ever be able to tell about days like today. Ahh, Ryan. I don't know anything about Ryan, I don't care. The man means nothing to me; he's just a name. But if going and finding him so he can go home, if that earns me the right to get back to my wife, well then that's my mission."

Captain Miller was willing to engage any conflict and endure any hardship if it meant being reunited with his wife. His mission was to return to her.

I desire you
As I desire no other.

From the moment I saw you
To the first time I kissed you
To the last second we shared together
You are the flame that burns deep within
And the light by which my life begins

In early days you framed my day
Brightened it as I awoke
Heightened it as I marched in
Now you are the art itself
Portrait of all that holds my gaze
The color and depth of all my days.

I don't know how you do it.
No class teaches this depth,
No column advises such grace.
You simply are.
You give yourself to me,
And receive from me freely.

My soul is vacant when we are apart
As one checks into a room not their own
But in seeing you I am home.
With you I am free of the mundane

Boredom is the domain of the disconnected
But passion is the familiar of the united.

My body hungers and craves yours
Our union the reality of my dream
Your closeness the blanket of my sleep.
When we share each other
I am never more aware of life
And never more at peace from strife.

I love you
As I love no other.

The FUN Coach: Mutuality

Selfish makes two. Selfless makes one.

1. Submission means to receive fully from each other. When is the last time you submitted? What did your partner have of worth to offer? How does this definition help your understanding of God's desire for your marriage?

2. Recall the last conflict you had in communication. How much of it was failure to listen to the emotion behind the words? Think of the last time you felt understood by your partner. Was it more their agreement with your words or their support of your feelings?

3. Conflict is often a difference in belief, interpretation or expectation.

    • What is a major belief difference between the two of you? In the text we talked about a partner who believes silence is bad and the other believes silence is a sign of security. Here's another example. One person believes admitting a person other than their spouse is attractive is honest and healthy. The other person believes it is disrespectful and promotes insecurity. Think of past conflicts. Which of them were due to different beliefs you didn't realize you had?

- When was the last time you and your partner interpreted an event differently? What was the fear behind the difference in interpretation?

- What different expectations have you discovered?

4. When you read about other voices you hear, such as the controlling father or critical mother, what came to mind? Whose voice do you associate with certain points of shame or fear? Review the work you did after chapter one when you identified shame and fears. Can you match a person to those? Consider the opposite: When you think of your desires and longings, do you associate a positive voice? Someone who was a champion or cheerleader for you with that quality?

5. Starting well involves focusing on the problem itself, identifying the fear behind it, stating a desired outcome and staying focused on one issue at a time. Recall a conversation that didn't go well. Which of these would have helped most? Is one of these more difficult than the others for you to communicate?

6. When was the last time one of you was guilty of avoidance? Which of the start- well practices would help alleviate the reason for your avoidance?

7. Mutuality is disrupted by blame, comparison and competition, nagging, insecurity, jealousy and sexual division. Which of these are sources of harm to your relationship? What is the next best thing you can do to protect against them?

8. Your mission is to return to your partner. What thoughts come to mind as you consider what that looks like?

Big Bang Theories

Recently, my wife and I celebrated Christmas for the first time by ourselves. Our children were out of town; our extended family lives away. For dinner, we decided to go out. We discovered that not much is open on Christmas Day. We also found out that reservations would have been a good idea.

We arrived at a nice steak and seafood restaurant. The wait for tables was long, so we strolled through the bar area. All the tables were filled but one. We squeezed into it. Next to us, very close to us, were two young women.

My wife and I ordered and as we waited for our food we held hands across the table and talked. At one point, the young woman next to me interrupted us.

"I'm sorry," she said, "but how long have you two been married?"

"Thirty years," I said.

"Wow. I would have guessed you had only been married a couple years the way you look at each other and hold hands. What do you do?"

"I'm a sex therapist."

The looks on their face was awesome, and I almost got away with it until they glanced at my wife.

"No, you are not!" they laughed.

"I am," I said. "I have one client. And she is very satisfied!"

Too amazing for words is the way of a man with a woman. The word *way* not only described a couple's journey but also their sexual union.

An entire book in the Bible, The Song of Songs (also known as Song of Solomon) is a Near Eastern love poem. Referred to as the finest of songs, The Song uses simile and metaphor to tastefully capture the strongest and intimate emotions and acts of sexual love.

The poem is written in chiastic structure. This is critically important for understanding the Song's force. A chiasm is a structure in which the themes and lines of the first half of the poem are identical to the themes and lines of the second half. A chiastic structure looks like this: ABCDDCBA. "D" is the point everything builds to and from which the rest flows. It is the whole point of the poem or story.

In Song of Songs, for example, the first four verses have the theme of "take me away." The second theme is "friends speak." The third theme is "my own vineyard." At the end of the Song, the last three themes correspond: my vineyard, friends speak and lastly, "come away." The Song comes full circle.

So what event does the Song work up to and from which all else flows? I'm not going to tell you yet. But I'm building to it.

Romance and sex is important enough God inspired a whole song about it and said, "Put that in my book."

It's important enough it's made its way in this book.

A man and woman marry. She has dreamed of this relationship. Dolls and kitties and doggies have all been dressed up as brides or grooms or attendants. Magazines have been earmarked and torn. She and friends have planned their weddings years in advance. She has imagined her family and house and vacations. Most of all, she has thought of him: Her man, her prince. When he kisses her, her heart beats a skip. When he holds her, she is assured. When she adorns sexy lingerie and teases him with seduction, his strength melts. He possesses her; she possesses him.

He, too, has looked for her. When he found her, he hoped he could win her. When he won her, he wonders how he will measure up for her. Every man believes he married out of his league. He sees her heart as precious, and when she opens it to him he is protective, as one is with treasure. He sees her body as the Holy Grail, the fountain of youth, the temple of the privileged. When she opens it to him, he is submerged, rewarded and renewed.

Why must it end? "How much the wife is dearer than the bride," Lord Lyttleton said. Honeymoons are supposed to end. Marriages are supposed to grow. Young lovers are rookies; mature lovers wear the rings of champions.

Putting the O in Romance

Every marriage desires more. No marriage, in which two love the other, is satisfied with dying embers of romance and sexual love. Circumstances change, adjustments are made; but the fire burns within and longs to spread.

Popular thought, conventional understanding and unquestioned teaching have doused the flames. Male and female has been victim. Both have been misunderstood regarding who they are and what they seek. Ironically, the Song has had it right for all these years. Observation, science, studies, technology: They all confirm the passionate resolve of the man and woman in the Song who are driven by desire, uninhibited with expression and inseparable in life.

Misunderstanding men and women when it comes to sexual desire is like keeping your thumb over the opening of a garden hose when the water is on. It's a mess, it's not getting the water where it needs to be and eventually you need to let go or turn off the water. Many couples turn off the water. I want you to let go and enjoy the flow.

We know some things.

Men's and women's brains have anatomical, chemical and functional differences. These differences are in regions that affect language, memory, emotion, vision, hearing and navigation. Researchers are still trying to figure out how these differences relate to many aspects of our behavior. They are especially still figuring out how it relates to sexual behavior.

The amygdala is larger in men. The amygdala has to do with emotion, emotional memory and mediating emotional behavior. It responds to sensory input and influences physiological response including sexual behavior. The smaller amygdala and the accompanying reduced serotonin levels may explain why anxiety disorder and depression is more common in women than men. However, the part that regulates emotions is smaller in men.

A man's medial preoptic is twice the size of a woman's. In the words of Carolyn Evans, it's where "hot happens." Apparently, men have a larger sexual real estate. But what that means is inconclusive.

Most of us have heard that men are more visual than women. Recent research indicates otherwise. A study was conducted with men and women viewing sexual stimuli. Each subject was to report if they found the stimulus arousing. At the same time, their physiological reaction was being monitored. For men the results were the same. If their body said they were turned on, their self-report agreed. People concluded that if a man has a physical reaction, he has a psychological reaction. What a man feels, he must act on.

It was different for women in the test. When their body said they were turned on, their self-report disagreed. There seemed to be a body-mind disconnect. Some supposed the difference was related to gender. Others wondered if women felt free to self-report honestly or if they were conditioned by cultural expectation.

Another test was conducted. This time women were divided into three groups. One gave their self-report to another student for review. Another was assured their answers would be anonymous. A third group was hooked up to what they believed was a polygraph. Physiologically, the results were the same. The difference was in the self-report. The self-report did not change for women who gave their result to a student. Mind denied body. However, the anonymous group admitted to being turned on more than they did previously. The third group changed their self-report significantly. Their mind reportedly agreed with their body. And their results were very similar to the men.

Teri Fisher summed up the study: "Being a human who is sexual, who is allowed to be sexual, is a freedom accorded by society much more readily to males than to females."

My wife has been telling me this for years. The visual stirs up sexual desire regardless of gender. The woman in our Song has been saying it all along for centuries.

There are, however, distinct qualities between men and women.

Love Her Body

A woman's body is built for her pleasure both physically and psychologically. For instance, the clitoris has no known purpose other than pleasure. Its eighteen parts comprising head, shaft and base extend through the pelvic area with 8000 nerve endings which is twice more than the male penis. The clitoris is an arousal network able to produce multiple orgasms in a single session.

Each orgasm releases oxytocin, a hormone that generates feelings of bond and trust and increases endorphins. Endorphins are linked with emotions of generosity, relief from pain and promotion of better sleep. Oxytocin increases fourfold during orgasm.

A woman's brain reacts differently than a man's brain in orgasm. The woman's brain goes silent, as if in a momentary trance; women have no emotional feeling in the ten to twenty seconds of their actual orgasm. It is lights out; she's in her own world. Then, with the release of oxytocin, it is light on; *you* are her world.

Though a woman's body is built for her pleasure, couples face two common problems. She is tired and she is easily distracted.

Carolyn Evans wrote a book called Forty Beads. It's a great read (and trust me, men, you want your partner to have this book). I remember when I first saw it. I skimmed it and set it down. The little I read stayed with me so I went back to the bookstore and read it in one setting. As I read, I thought, "I can't believe a woman is writing this." I bought it and took it home.

After writing about the extremes of women who love, love, love sex versus women who hate, hate, hate, sex, she talks about the majority:

> We like sex, but we probably crave a lot of other things a lot more. And while we definitely can appreciate all the benefits that the toe-curling, mind-blowing orgasm delivers, we're also okay with a good book, a warm blanket, and a dark chocolate Dove Bar…The thing is, for us women, sometimes sex is all starbursts and fireworks, and other times it's just okay. And while we might be unclear on what our outcome will be, there's one thing we know for sure: There's going to be clean-up involved…Throw in all the other demands placed on our time in any given 24-hour period, and sex easily gets pushed to the tail end of our to-do list."

Women desire sex. No question. Their desires have been constrained and misrepresented. She thinks you are hot. You send her quivering. But there is a difference between low desire and a slow build up. Often what you think of as low desire is physical exhaustion. I write later about how to help her receive the physical and emotional connection she craves more than a chocolate bar.

Back to the brain: The amygdala and prefrontal cortex process fear and anxiety. They need to be less active during sex in order for women to engage and reach their peak. A woman has to feel safe before she can go lights out in her head let alone in your room. Safety is both contextual and relational.

Contextual safety has to do with your environment. Are the kids going to come in? (Men, buy a lock.) Is there more work to be done before she can call it a day? (Men, *git r done*). Will her mother drop by? (Men, hire security).

Relational safety has to do with emotions. Loss of connection reduces desire; reduced desire means less sex; less sex means hurt feelings. The answer is sex. Most therapists agree: It takes sex to want sex. But women are not wired to be scared off and turned on at the same time. Affirmation is the bridge back.

A woman's body is built for pleasure more than a man's body. Overcome fatigue and distraction and you've got yourself a sexual quake ready to rumble, a volcano of desire ready to erupt, a (well, you get it).

Write Her Story

Women love stories. Traditional romance novel sales approach 1.5 billion dollars per year. On the web, fan fiction, frequented mostly by women, holds over two million stories and has 600,000 visitors per day. Most of those visitors are young women 18-24 years old.

A typical romance plot sees the heroine overcoming obstacles to win the heart of and marry the man who is right for her. It is all about choice of mate. The woman is the central character. Her desire is for the desire of the man. She is the object of his admiration.

In the Song, you have three primary voices: the woman, the man, and the friends. The primary figure is the woman. She has the most lines. The interaction with the friends is primarily hers. Most of the man's lines sing of her beauty.

If a woman senses that the man has made career or sport or hobby or obsession central to the story, she will rewrite the script.

In their story, women want what is prized and what is potent. The woman prizes relationship with you characterized by togetherness and tenderness. She also longs to be the object of your passionate need, to feel her power. Both build up her plot. She will tell her friends her story.

So, husband, what is her story? Does it comprise the prized and the potent? Give her friends a reason to sing.

Flare With Flair

Men are artists. Typically, we are told that men are hunters and women are the object of their hunt: Lure, sack, trophy.

But men are created to mine the beautiful and the exquisite. When Adam was placed in the garden, it was to work it and take care of it. Do you think he was weeding? The account describes trees of beauty, flowing rivers, natural watering sources. Adam was there to shape what was. He was a partner with God in imagining and creating what could be.

Excavating the exquisite is man's creative drive. All men have flair. The chef draws on flavors and designs a picture-perfect meal. The architect imagines what materials arranged and combined together could make. An athlete maximizes muscular potential. The police officer promotes the peace of law and order. Even the hunter is exquisite in plan and execution. Men pour themselves in to draw the best.

The problem for men is the pressure to perform. Artistry succumbs to the reality their work is subject to evaluation. It makes the grade or it does not. This affects their romantic and sexual heart. "The male problem with sexuality is due to his sensitivity to shame. Women like to think of themselves as being sexually desirable or sexual attractors. Men like to think of themselves as being sexual performers. Womanhood is rarely at stake in a sexual encounter." Patricia Love

Under pressure to perform, a man sacrifices discovering the woman's sexual gold to measuring up to standards of sexual performance. But all men know gold is better than any passing grade. Keep the "A." I'll take her "O."

In the fiber of their being, in the depth of their desire, a man wants to please the woman sexually. There is no greater affirmation than the look of exquisite agony in a woman's orgasm, the tension and contraction of her body, the ferocious clinging after as she seeks to hold him closer than is physically possible. Orgasm, of course, isn't the only treasure. The sheer fact that his woman desires his desire, that regardless of outcome her beauty is tapped, satisfies his need to pour in and create.

Give Him a Top Ten

Whereas women love stories, men love highlights. It's not that men don't enjoy stories, but there is a reason Sports Center is so popular. Few guys say, "Hey, unless I can watch the whole game I don't want to see what happened."

It's also why men like action-adventure movies. There isn't a lot of plot or character development. Dialogue is only necessary to set up the next big boom.

Tests bear this out. One experiment used boy and girl monkeys as subjects. Boy monkeys chose to play with trucks, girl monkeys chose to play with dolls. I suspect some boy monkeys played with dolls: What else would the truck run over?

A similar test was conducted with human boys and girls. Boys chose toys that could be propelled through space or that promoted rough and tumble play. Girls played with toys they could nurture.

Another test, this with one-year old boys and girls, demonstrated that girls look at their mother more than boys do; and shown film of faces or cars, girls watched faces and boys watched cars.

To see if these results were due to conditioning or nature, a test was conducted with one-day old boys and girls. They were shown the picture of a friendly face or a mobile. The mobile the same color, size and shape but the face had its features scrambled. Girls preferred the face; boys preferred the mobile.

Men like a good story, but they love the highlight. The day after a game, most guys don't ask their friend, "What did you think of the game?" They ask, "Did you see that play?" And when a guy likes an actual book, ask his favorite part. There's a boom factor.

Women provide men their highlight. I'm not saying your man will put it out there for his friends to see. It's enough for him to know he has a highlight. And maybe for his friends to know he has a highlight they will never see. Give him something to talk about, even if he remains silent to protect the not so innocent.

A woman lives in a story that comprises all she prizes. Her desire is to be desired by her man and admired by her friends.

A man seeks to mine beauty that reflects his doing. He is inspired by the reward of his number one fan.

The man writes his lover's story. The woman inspires her man's creativity. Their romance consists of four prized, potent and highlight-worthy dynamics: D.U.I.T.

- Draw
- Uncover
- Intercourse
- Thrill

(Say it with me: Just DUIT).

Draw

Both men and women desire more romance. More men than women surveyed wish their partner was more romantic. Would you have guessed that?

Couples in their first five years hold hands more than any other group. Less than half of couples married over twenty years hold hands regularly.

Passionate kissing declines with age. It doesn't have to. Overall more than half of married couples never or rarely kiss with passion. More than half of couples with kids never or rarely do so. Maybe that's why nearly two thirds of couples married ten to twenty years never or rarely kiss with wild abandon.

These are statistics. They are not the desire. The survey says *romance me*.

Draw transforms a person's world. It reminds your partner of the paradise of your relationship. Your lover often lives outside their favorite world. They are captive to responsibility and urgency, confined by expectation and caught off guard by the unexpected. Draw returns them home.

The Beloved in the Song sings "Kiss me for your love is more delightful than wine. Pleasing is the fragrance of your perfumes…Listen, it's my lover!

Look! Here he comes…My lover spoke and said to me 'Arise and come with me.' Your love causes me to lose all composure."

We draw our lover to us with three magnetic practices:

1. Arousal and anticipation
2. Chase and play
3. Take and steal away

Love does not outgrow infatuation; infatuation blossoms within mature love. During infatuation, you and your lover experience an altered state of consciousness. Little or no blood flows to the neo-cortex, the rational part of your brain. You are out of your mind. You are transported from the world you were in to the world you long to be in.

The Beloved sings of her lover's taste and scent. Betsy Prioleau writes:

> In desire the senses claim us first. A touch, a scent, a gaze, a hoarse vibrato can make our hearts do handsprings. Later, cerebral charms take over and summon the serious passions…In the first three or four seconds of meeting a man, a woman will subject him to a face scan, spending 75% of the time on his mouth and eyes. Within five minutes she will have sized him up…A smile is a female sweet spot. *Swoon*

Arousal leads your lover from a sense of where they are (busy, distracted, feeling neglected) to senses they long to possess. Your touch lingers; your eyes hold and invite; a tailored smile embraces the spirit. Tone of voice changes climate. "You have stolen my heart with one glance of your eyes" the Lover tells his Beloved.

Arousal plays the keyboard of affirmation. It sounds the notes of emotional attachment. It calls to the beauty of your partner to arise.

When you arouse your partner, you leverage the sensual to key into their deepest longing. Do they desire to be respected? What do they hear, see, smell, taste, experience – their favorite or yours? Do they long to be admired? Who is asking more questions – you or them? Whose perspective is being affirmed?

The Beloved responds to her lover's attention. Molly Peacock describes the sensation of being the man's focus "as if you were a camouflaged animal in a forest being found."

The Song is an exchange of words. When women talk, they experience a chemical rush second only to what they experience in orgasm. When a man talks with a woman, he does more than connect verbally; he literally taps into her pleasure.

On average, girls aged 12-17 send and receive 80 texts per day; boys the same age send and receive 30 (mostly to and from girls is my guess). 59% of the girls talk on their cell every day compared to 42% of boys.

One survey concluded the strongest indicator of sexual and marital satisfaction for women was the ability to express sexual feelings to their husbands. The more they talked, the better they rated their sex lives, marriages and overall happiness. Sounds like a fun subject to me.

Ovid, the Roman poet, said, "Women are conquered by eloquent words." Perhaps that's why surveys indicate women prefer a man's intelligence over his beauty or wealth; or why 3500 women worldwide said poetry was a man's third most persuasive dynamic in romance. Betsy Prioleau says "Female sexuality is flattery operated."

Men are moved by words as well. Remember, intimate talk produces a higher physiological reaction in men. He is being invited to be himself: To pour in and to draw from.

For men, arousal and anticipation stimulates the physical and the possible. His heart for action-adventure has been put on alert. When a man feels he acts.

In the Song, the Lover says, "My dove in the cleft of the rock, in the hiding places on the mountainside, show me your face and let me hear your voice. Catch for us the foxes, the little foxes that ruin the vineyards, our vineyards that are in blossom." Some people interpret catching the foxes as fixing problems in a relationship. Maybe it's the opposite. Hide and seek; running carefree – these are pictures of lovers at play.

Man and woman hold mystery in their heart. They long to be known, to be loved by one who wants to know more. Lovers hide but they do not hide out; they respond to the sincere call to show their self. No one plays hide and seek in hopes they are left abandoned.

Too often, the dying embers of romance fade on the false contentment there is nothing more to be known about each other.

 Chase and play attunes our emotional bond. Intimacy is a circle. We often start by disclosing facts and surface feelings. We move to sharing longings and fears. As we become aware of deeper core fears we are able to respond to satisfy the longing. Every day new facts and feelings are exchanged; and if we listen, we hear the longings and the fears within them.

Every person at all times is playing hide and seek. No one plays to be left behind.

How does your lover want to be known? What do they want you to call out from them? Play reveals. Game-on excites. Our lover is stuck in the classroom of life. Draw rings the bell for recess.

40% of women reported to Cosmo that their partners were never or not very romantic. 75% of men said they are consistently romantic. What is the discrepancy?

Romance is more than flower and chocolate or dinner and date night. Draw builds anticipation. Play signals that more to her story is being written. Play suggests a highlight is in the making.

True play builds to satisfy your partner's longing. It attends to their deeper emotion. Sometimes it really is the gift that counts. You thought about them: they feel cherished. At times all one wants is to be held: to feel safe. Quickies can be a highlight too: they feel wanted. Either plan or spontaneity may be just right: they feel valued.

Do you remember recess in school? Did you play the same game every day? Always speaking in your partner's love language can be like playing the same game at recess. What if we think in terms of a love map instead? They might be in a different place. You may be playing soccer and they want to swing from the monkey bars. Play discovers where they want to be and takes them there.

Early Christians were told "It is better to marry than to burn with passion."

"Come with me," the Lover calls.

"Take me away," the Beloved cries. "Bring me into your chamber. Come my Lover, let us spend the night in the villages; at our door is every delicacy that I have stored up for you."

Studies and surveys of female fantasy consistently report their desire to be sexually irresistible and ravished. She does not want to be taken against her will. She does want to willingly comply and to give in to her lover's passion for her that is so intense it shatters constraints.

The book *Fifty Shades of Grey* set the record as the fastest-selling paperback of all time, eclipsing the *Harry Potter* series. It is a novel with themes of bondage and discipline, dominance and submission. Critics are many and the opposition is loud: they call out the moral message and advocate for women's safety. Of course, omen everywhere want to be safe and want their body to be respected. So why have women made the book a bestseller?

One survey revealed that 90% of men's sex dreams involved the woman initiating sex. Men are in on this too? Men need to feel irresistible and ravished?

One woman said, "What I miss is the high I felt when he and I were first dating. A year after we were married, the familiarity set in and the excitement went away. I'd do anything to get that back. I don't want another man. He's everything I want. I just wish we could meet all over again and feel that intensity." *Hot Monogamy*

We desire to be desired. That's the reality of being built for community: mutual longing.

We want to hear a person say to us, "Your love causes me to lose all composure."

Low sex drives affect men and women. One therapist said low sex drive in men may be a silent epidemic leaving women suffering in silent confusion and depression. Women's sex drive often needs a jump start to turn on their libido. The jump start they need is display of avid desire: arouse, chase, and take. Draw lights the fire. The burn begins.

To steal away isn't necessarily literal. The Beloved speaks of how their bed is luxuriant. The Lover says the beams of their house are cedar, also a luxury. They may be speaking of their house, literally, or are celebrating how the scene of their love is idyllic. The emphasis is on the setting that reflects their love. Drawing our lover into the place they want to be, we are swept from the mundane to an exalted elsewhere. Distraction is vanquished. Possibility is aroused. Recess nears. Satisfaction of deep desire is promised. The fear of emotional disconnection is alleviated. Low desires shift into motion. High passions burn freely. Love is in place. It's time to raise the roof.

Uncover

Two are drawn. Within, they feel the affirmation of the other. Closeness is upon them. The depth of knowing each other again and more invites them to leave all else behind. They are removed from another world and returned to their own. They are taken and together.

Still there is a veil. Insecurity lurks in one's spirit as a stowaway. Like the Beloved of the Song, we are aware of our appearance: "Do not stare at what the sun has done" she says. But insecurity haunts more than the physical. The Beloved has two dreams. "I looked for him but did not find him," she said. "I opened the door for my lover, but my lover left. My heart sank at his departure." Behind two dreams is one question: Am I the desire of the moment or the desire of a lifetime?

Words of the Song are notes of praise for the character and attributes of the other. The Song is a symphony of desire focused on a relationship that is unparalleled and inseparable.

The Beloved says of her Lover that his name is perfume. Name spoke of character, perfume as that which emanates. His reputation is extravagant. "No wonder the maidens love you," she says. She has told her story and spread his fame. When she describes his arms as rods of gold she speaks of his nobility and worth.

When the Lover likens her neck to the tower of David he is commending her strength. No man could just take her; her love is a gift. He repeats his description of her in another stanza to assure her that his admiration is not diminished. He refers to her as the cities of Tirzah and Jerusalem, two cities of power and splendor. Then he requests that she turn her eyes for they overwhelm him

Two-thirds of men surveyed said they want women to compliment them on an intangible quality they uniquely possess. The Beloved tells her Lover you are as regal as the King and only you can stir up such extravagant feeling.

Each other's confidence is fortified. They speak in comparisons. "You are like a mare harnessed to one of the chariots of Pharaoh," says the Lover. Such horses were decorated with ornaments and embroidery, symbolic of beauty and dignity. "You are a lily among thorns," he adds. She returns the comparison: "Like an apple tree among the forest is my lover among the young men. I delight to sit in his shade and his fruit is sweet to my taste." He is the one from whom she derives relief and pleasure.

One woman asked, "If my husband always wants 'it' when does he want me?" The Beloved and Lover make clear: "My desire is you." It's a vital distinction. Physical sex drive is not the measure of desire itself.

I was recently diagnosed with low testosterone. Before I knew of the issue, I had a couple instances of lovemaking with my wife where I couldn't climax. She had no problem. The medical community says low testosterone can result in low sexual desire. I said to my wife, "I don't understand that. My desire for you is no less. I want you all the time. My body just won't do what I want." Don't worry though. After treatment, I'm good to go again. Thank you for asking. Thank you, doctor.

Lovers treat the other as their equal and undress them as their superior. When insecurities are adorned in admiration, real garments fall. The lovers look upon each other with unabashed pleasure.

The Beloved captures her lover's physique in terms of strength and value. She describes his cheeks like beds of spice and his lips like lilies; she tells him of the effect of his kisses. She is not just looking at him. She is feeling him. She makes his body hers. She describes his head of hair and looks into his eyes. She kisses him and strokes his arms. She runs her hands down his body, bends her knees as she traces her touch along his legs. She rises and joins her mouth to his. "Your mouth is sweetness itself."

The Lover speaks of his beloved's appearance in three different stanzas of the Song. He uses similar imagery but with different intent. The first time, he describes how he feels when he looks at her. He looks her over from head to feet and asserts: "All beautiful you are, my darling, there is no flaw in you." Then he tells her is going to take her to him "until the day breaks and the shadows flee." The second stanza is continued affirmation of his admiration and how she rises above all others. The final stanza is spoken in the course of his bringing her pleasure.

The Lover, this time, begins with her sandaled feet, removing them with the care and honor one would do with a princess. His hands glide up her thighs as he praises their form and artistry. He settles upon her vulva (*navel* is a poorer translation) as lips upon a goblet of wine; his mouth moves upon her waist as one who seeks nourishment from the field. He delights her breasts with caresses as tender as one would pet two fawns. The Lover kisses her neck, lingering on her smooth feel, and then brings his eyes to her. This time he does not ask her to turn them away. He dives into them as deep pools. Her nose brings to her face portion and balance, and he nestles his against hers as one finally home. His fingers trail down her hair. He promises to consume her.

Couples uncover insecurity and adorn it with affirmation. They uncover bodies and clothe them with verbal and physical praise. The lover knows a woman's fear and anxiety must be alleviated. It only takes 250 milliseconds for a hint of rejection to trigger one's brain process, and only a quarter of a second to try to make sense of the perceived rejection. The marriage bed is to be each other's safe haven.

Without distractions, a woman can be aroused in thirty seconds. What is the number one distraction? Over half of women surveyed are dissatisfied with their bodies; nearly two-thirds have felt distracted due to worrying about how their body looks.

Three-fourths of men surveyed said they are satisfied with their partner's breast size. The other fourth are idiots. The Lover says in the Song "May your breasts be like the clusters of the vine, the fragrance of your breath like apples and your mouth like the best wine." The likely translation of breath is actually nipples. He finds her sweet to his taste and intoxicating.

Women are not alone in physical concerns. Many men are insecure about the size of their penis. They can relax. One study was conducted to analyze the hundred most common physical descriptors used to describe the hero in romance novels. No synonym for penis appeared anywhere. The seven most frequent masculine features are cheekbones, jaw, brows, shoulder, forehead, waist and hips. The one universal asset women look to the most: his butt.

Affirmation is show and tell.

Women have more sensitive skin than men. Touch is at the forefront of their sexual desire. Greater lovers believe in slow sex movement.

Kisses are turbocharged touches. The lips are densely populated with sensory neurons. Kisses trigger chemicals that transmit closeness and euphoria. The kiss activates motivation and reward regions of the brain, boosts pulse and blood pressure and deepens breathing. Rational thought retreats. Scarlett O'Hara said, "You should be kissed, and often, and by someone who knows how."

The Lover ensures his Beloved is central to the story. She prizes his desire for her and she revels in the power she has over him.

The Beloved, once insecure, grows confident in her beauty and in her belonging. The Lover pours himself in to mine all that makes her exquisite.

In turn, she tells her friends her story and makes him the hero.

Intercourse

"He has taken me to the banquet hall and his banner over me is love. Strengthen me with raisins, refresh me with apples, for I am faint with love. His left arm is under my head, and his right arm embraces me."

The Beloved is saying, "I am intoxicated with his intention. He spreads me out on the bed, his arms holding and pleasuring me."

She says also, "My lover is mine and I am his; he browses among the lilies." He partakes of the pleasures she offers.

The Song is a chiasm. The first half of the poem leads to the central theme from which all else flows. The center is the theme. What does the Song build to?

> Beloved: Awake, north wind, and come, south wind! Blow on my garden that its fragrance may spread abroad. Let my lover come into his garden and taste its choice fruits.

> Lover: I have come into my garden, my bride; I have gathered my myrrh with my spice, I have eaten my honeycomb and my honey; I have drunk my wine and my milk.

> Friends: Eat, O friends, and drink; be drunk with lovemaking.

The song builds to their intercourse.

Intercourse is natural but the heart and art of intercourse makes it masterful.

The Beloved calls out the winds so that her fragrance may draw the Lover to herself. She invites him to enjoy her fully. He responds with poetic exhilaration. He has consumed her. The beloved's friends sing the chorus that would rival any rendition of Handel's Messiah. Some Jewish historians have suggested that the voice here is not that of friends but of God.

Over the years, an act of divine intoxication has been sobered by misuse. As one comedian says, "Banging, nailing and screwing isn't sex; it's carpentry." Religious advocates have done no better than carnal libertines. Both have relegated sexual pleasure to the confines of limited thinking and have bound it to chains of restriction or regret.

Intercourse is artistry. The Song celebrates the full dimension of intercourse:

- Awakening
- Intoxication
- Entry
- Possession
- Blessing

Our bodies harmonize with the other. Waves of readiness wash across us. Two become one, and in their release, chemicals bathe their very being with union. God speaks his favor.

A woman's vagina is 3-4 inches in length. It can double in size during sexual excitement. Her clitoris has eight thousand nerve endings, the majority of which are concentrated on the surface of the vulva. A woman is able to orgasm without any vaginal penetration. The inner two-thirds of her vagina are less sensitive than the outer third. A woman's genitals are self-cleaning and more sanitary than many other parts of her body.

When men spend 20 minutes or more on foreplay, including manual or oral pressure on their lover's vulva, 92% of women reach orgasm consistently.

Prior to orgasm, during the awakening and intoxication phase, women will experience increases in their pace of breathing, body temperature and heart rate. She will feel tension in her muscles including tightening of her abdominal muscles and throbbing of her PC muscles. She will sense a bearing down on her pelvic area.

As she orgasms, her vagina and uterus will contract ten to fifteen times for just under a second each. Her rectal sphincter will contract two to five times. Her breathing will race and her pulse will quicken to 110-180 beats per minute. Though the entire process will last several minutes, the orgasm itself is a ten to twenty second experience. Many men confuse the growing waves of her orgasm as the climax itself. It is not. The orgasm is distinctly different in experience. It changes the momentum that builds to it. Muscles throughout her body will tense and release in spasms. An orgasm is a jolt.

Women have described the experience as going into an altered state (Remember: Her brain has no emotional feeling: Lights out). One woman said "It is about strength and at the same time the vulnerability of being so close to him."

Wonderfully, women may orgasm repeatedly. As great lovers say, give her a double before you finish your single.

Of all the sexual positions, men and women still both prefer the man on top. It's hard to replicate the closeness, the eye contact, the exchange of breath the position promotes. However, it's not naturally the most satisfying position physically for a woman. When she is on top, she can lean back slightly and control the pressure of her clitoris against the man's pubic bone. The man supplies the pressure and she controls the rhythm and pace.

When the man is on top, he can promote a better experience for her by penetrating from a higher angle so that the head of his penis moves in contact with the first two inches inside the top of her vagina. The man places pressure on the woman's clitoris with the base of his penis and pubic bone. Maintaining contact with the clitoris, the man wants to shift his weight forward and engage in more rocking and rotation than thrusting.

The man is built to please his lover. The average size of a flaccid penis is 2.4-3.5 inches. Flaccid size has nothing to do with the size of his erection. 76% of erect penises measure 4.5-6.25 inches; the average is 5.1 inches and has a diameter of 1.6 inches. A man's ejaculate will travel 28 mph. Average ejaculate is a teaspoon in volume and its main ingredient is fructose: 5 calories, 6mg protein, 60% recommended daily dose of Vitamin C. The man will experience 4-8 contractions during his orgasm.

Intercourse is amazing. Lovers are worlds away but in their own world. Lights out but lit up.

But not all is bright. According to Psychology Today, the average sex session is between 3-10 minutes. Not that couples don't enjoy an occasional quickie, but considering it takes the average woman ten to twenty minutes to reach peak arousal, someone is getting shorted. That someone is the woman, half who admit they want sex to last longer and who say the worst mistake a man makes is not providing enough foreplay.

More foreplay is a woman's top wish followed by more romance and less predictability. They want spontaneous and fun.

Surprisingly, 44% of men say their partner doesn't communicate enough. In other words, he wants to know what pleases her. As one person said, "I'm not clairvoyant, tell me or show me." Men's top three wishes are more diversity in sexual experience, less passivity from the woman and more sounds of affirmation. Please keep it real.

Maybe it's the guy in me, but perhaps women would be more diverse and less passive if men met their three wishes first. Be the genie to bring out the genie.

Thrill

"Come, my lover," the Beloved says. "Let us go to the countryside. There I will give you my love. At our door is every delicacy, both new and old that I have stored up for you, my lover."

"His fruit is sweet to my taste...He browses among the lilies"

"You are a garden fountain," says the Lover. "You are a well of flowing water."

"May my wine go straight to my lover," she answers, "flowing gently over lips and teeth."

Both new and old, she promises. What you love and will always desire; what I will give that you have longed to try. Lovers want to swim in the delight of the familiar. Lovers seek to wade in fresh waters. Couples seek to keep it new so it's never through.

Romance and sex is thrill.

The point is not an endless parade of new positions and tricks of the trade. Those are often pointless charade. Exploration and discovery is the terrain of lovers. There is no such thing as trial and error. Love tries.

But thrill requires freedom and affirmation.

Most couples don't talk about sex, they talk around sex. One-third of women said they are thinking about sexual things they're embarrassed to talk about; one-fourth are imagining a sexual position she's afraid to ask her lover to try.

86% of men and women said they want to do something sexually with their partner they haven't done before.

Dr. Patricia Love says one question helps: "Is there anything you want me to do for you, something I have never done or haven't done in a long time?"

That's a great question.

Are you more afraid to ask or are you more afraid to be asked? My guess is most people are more afraid to be asked. We are happy to ask because we want to please. We are nervous to answer because we don't want to hurt feelings.

In our protection of each other (I don't want to hurt their feelings), we have sacrificed the trust of our emotional bond. For both to ask willingly and answer honestly affirms "I am for you and we are in this together."

Thrill isn't limited to trying out the new. Thrill thrives on depth. New or old, the thrill is in the power of intimacy.

Did you know 80% of men would love if their woman ambushed them with sex when they least expect it? Why? Affirmation: take and steal away.

Did you know 72% of women are turned on when a man helps around the house? Why? Because they are tired! And it's advocacy: we are in this together.

Did you know that the fastest growing sex toy consumer market is women over 40yrs old? I didn't know that either.

Romance and sex isn't about any one act. It's the bond. It's for a person to be drawn, uncovered, one in flesh and thrilled. You and your marriage were created for it.

Some people have questions about the appropriateness of certain sexual acts and expressions. A man named Paul, an early leader in the Christian church, asked three questions to help followers of Jesus make decisions:

- Is it lawful?
- Is it helpful?
- Does it control you?

God is clear on what is lawful: ""Love does no harm. Therefore love is the fulfillment of the law." It is lawful if it is done in love and does no harm.

God is clear on what is helpful: It promotes togetherness and banishes lone-ness.

God is clear on what frees you: It feeds your affirmation, acceptance and advocacy and starves your shame and fear. It promotes self-disclosure not secrecy, intimacy not intimidation, joy not judgment. It drives you to new-found heights it does not drag you to soul-torn lows. It puts a rhythm in your walk and a dance in your step. You minimize what others criticize because you've maximized what others have minimized. There's no going back, no slowing down, no veering off and no loss of direction. Forward is the only step you know to take.

Sex is to free you not enslave you. Only you as a couple can determine with honesty if an aspect of your romantic and sexual life serves your best or surfaces your worst. God intends for no one but his Spirit to dictate otherwise.

Across the Room

> I want you to see me
> Across the room
> As the look of my eyes
> Signal desire too great for words
> And too true for lies.
>
> I want each step we take
> Toward each other

To dance to the quickened
Beat of our heart as
Imagination and anticipation is hastened.

I want our outstretched
Hands to touch,
And in that moment
For spirits to soar, exhilaration
Silencing our once lonely lament.

In the embrace that follows,
The perfect fit of two
Pressed as one and yearning for more,
Passion and dream unite
And gaze above to the Lover's shore

I want to lead you to our room
Close the door, draw you to me
As the walls grow silent, ready to store
The sound of lovers released,
The crescendo of their finest score.

We rest, questions not extinguished
But doubts put to rest.
Sealed with kisses and tender embrace
We have walked across the room
Into our best other, our chosen place.

The FUN Coach: Sexuality

1. Give your romance and sexual life with your partner a general assessment. What is right? What needs improvement? What is missing? What questions are unresolved?

2. A woman's body is created for their pleasure. Women love stories. How do these two insights help you think about romance and sex differently than before? You can neglect her body by not giving her enough pleasure or by not alleviating tiredness and distraction. You can neglect her story by not casting her in the lead; by not making her the object of your greatest need. Which is the greater neglect: body or story?

3. A man is an artist who loves highlights. How has he mined the exquisite in you? How does he know? Think of the last time he had a grin on his face because of something you did? What was it? Why do you think it meant so much for him? What inner longing did it satisfy or what fear did it alleviate? What romantic or sexual highlight is next on his list – even if he can't air it to his friends?

4.   *Draw* involves romancing your partner through arousal, chase and take. Of the three, which would most add to your romantic life today? Which do you do best and your partner do best? Picture a "start-well" conversation about one of these: how would you focus on the issue and state a desired outcome while alleviating shame and fear?

5.   Uncover adorns insecurity with affirmation verbally and physically. Do you know any physical insecurity your partner clings to? What can you say or do to overcome it? Maybe your partner has obvious beauty, things others comment on. How is it more special to you? How can you make it personal and meaningful?

6.   Intercourse is natural but the heart and art behind it makes it masterful. Think of the review you did earlier on romance and sex in general. Now ask those questions of intercourse specifically. What is right or needs help or is missing or confusing? What do you need to address these – resources, a coach or an honest conversation? A whole song – which God put in his Bible – builds to intercourse as its dominant theme. How do you feel about that – affirmed, amused, sad, threatened? Why? Who can help?

7. Thrill asks "Is there anything you want me to do for you, something I have never done or haven't done in a long time?" Is your communication in a safe place for you to ask or be asked this question? What shame or fears might surface and how can you anticipate those? You might try this: Agree for each of you to ask and answer the question. Tell the other how what you want means so much to you coming from them. Express the longing being met. Now give it a day before you come together and commit. Agree that when you talk:

- You will discuss why you are hesitant to do something. Is it fear based or performance/skill based? Do you need conversation to alleviate the fear, understanding to wait or help in knowing what to do?

- When you commit to doing what they want, you affirm that their pleasure is your pleasure. Assure them they do not need to feel guilty for asking: you don't see their request as selfish but as a desire to be close.

8. If there is no harm and it promotes intimacy, enjoy. Any violation of conscience or fear of compulsive behavior requires conversation. What do you need to help resolve your concern?

Make It New To See It Through

I came up out of the water
Raised my hands up to the Father
Gave it all to Him that day
Felt a new wind kiss my face

Walked away eyes wide open
Could finally see where I was going
It didn't matter where I'd been
I'm not the same man I was then

I got off track I made mistakes
Backslid my way to that place
Where souls get lost, lines get crossed
And the pain won't go away
I hit my knees now here I stand
There I was now here I am
Here I am, changed

I got a lot of 'hey I'm sorrys'
For things I've done
Man that was not me
I wish that I could take it all back
I just want to tell 'em that

I'm changed for the better
More smiles, less bitter
I'm even starting to forgive myself
Yes I am

I hit my knees now here I stand
There I was now here I am
Here I am, here I am
I'm changed

I'm changed for the better
Thank God I changed
(Rascal Flatts)

The song resonates in us. Do you remember the time you got off track, made mistakes; the place where a line got crossed and your soul got lost? Can you think of the people you want to say "I'm sorry, that wasn't me; I wish I could take it back?"

Have you longed for a new wind to kiss your face?

You, your partner and your marriage can change for the better. It's the cry of my heart, the conviction of my writing and the commitment of my coaching. It's the message that is woven throughout FUN Marriage. Feel bound? Affirmation, acceptance and advocacy free you. Feel distant? Mystery, mutuality and sexuality unite you.

You possess worth. You belong. You are competent. Fear and shame no longer masters your behavior. Your partner chooses words and actions that mirror the true you. Your marriage is not just a gift to you both. It is a gift to the world. You are made new to make new.

Made New

The phrase *doubting Thomas* comes from a story related to a follower of Jesus named Thomas. When his friends said they saw Jesus resurrected after his death, he said, "Unless I see the nail marks in his hands and put my finger where the nails were, and put my hand into his side, I will not believe." A phrase was born.

But there is more to his story, just as there is more to yours.

Earlier Jesus told his friends he was going to a place where others had tried to kill him. Thomas said, "Let's go that we may die with him."

Another time, Jesus talked about going to prepare a place and then returning to his friends. Thomas spoke up, "We don't know where you are going."

Shortly before his death, Jesus' friends told him they would rather die with him than ever disown him. Thomas was among those who said it. Thomas couldn't bear the thought of being apart from Jesus. Thomas loved Jesus.

Then he deserted him. Every one of Jesus' friends deserted him. And then Jesus died.

Thomas suffered both failure and loss. Failure results in discouragement, disappointment and depression. It's the place where you are unsure of anything including yourself. Loss results in disillusionment. Ralph Waldo Emerson penned, "For of all sad words of tongue or pen, the saddest are these: It might have been."

Thomas' doubt wasn't just intellectual it was emotional. You can hear it in the graphic use of his words: "unless I touch where the nails drove through and the sword pierced."

A week later, he was back in the house with his friends. The first time, when Jesus appeared, he wasn't where he was supposed to be. He was on his own, buried in his disappointment and disillusionment.

Jesus shows up. He says to Thomas "See and touch." Then he says, "Stop doubting and believe." Thomas did. The rest of his life would be in wild pursuit of his love for Jesus.

You married with no eye on separation. Love means together. In the course of your marriage, you have possibly suffered failure and loss. You try to work through discouragement. You try not to camp in disillusionment.

Perhaps as well you are not where you are supposed to be. But you have decided to turn your heart toward home. That's why you've read this far. You want to enter into the waters of cleansing and emerge hands upraised. You turn to receive the kiss of new beginning.

Every marriage desires more. So does every person. "Forgetting what is behind," the apostle Paul declared, "I press on to take hold of that for which Jesus took hold of me." God's love is relentless and his grace is bottomless. More is always what God has in store. He has it for you and he has it for your marriage.

Made new is to receive. Make new is to give. We love because God first loved us. It always works this way: God initiates, shapes and enables. We rally to his lead, craft his work and drive it with power not our own to completion. God works in us and then through us. He gives to us and we give away. In and out; in and out: It's called breath. Breath means you have a future to realize. It might be a day's worth or decade's worth, but the future is there and there is more in it.

It's possible to skip being made new and jump straight to make new. It means you will have passed on what God has to offer. You will rally to designs of your own making; you will craft with your own skill and ingenuity. You will drive yourself on one long breath until you can hold it no longer. Along the way, God will continue to invite you into his plan. You may do well on your own: you were created in his image after all. But there will always be the more he has in store.

Thomas learned that failure and loss isn't the end. The risen Jesus is living testimony to an unstoppable God.

Thomas also learned that one practice is essential to realizing more: Stop doubting and believe. To understand this practice fully, walk with me to a mountain. The time is shortly after the resurrection of Jesus. His close followers and some 500 others have already seen him alive again. The eleven he had poured his life into go to meet him. He appears, and it says they worshiped him but some doubted.

Their doubt was not intellectual. Jesus is in front of them. Their eyes do not lie.

The word translated doubted means hesitated. That makes sense. The unstoppable God was about to send them on a life-long adventure in which they would realize the more in store. This was no longer preparation. It was real. It was now. Some weren't sure.

Return again to these words: stop doubting and believe. Believe is not intellectual; it is actual. Belief joins in.

To be made new and make new means to leave your hesitation behind and join in:

1. What God leads, you rally to.
2. What God shapes, you craft.
3. What God enables, you drive.

Make New

People cling to two myths about change.

Myth 1: People don't like change.

Actually, people love change.

Just this morning, I changed my socks. I also changed out of my silk, Incredible Hulk boxer shorts. I showered (changing my scent) and I shaved (changing my appearance). I love change.

I used to be single. Once, I even took a test that predicted I had the gift of celibacy. Then I met my wife. I ex*changed* my gift of celibacy for the gift of marriage. I love change.

My wife and I used to be without children. We enjoyed sleep. I enjoyed being a neat freak borderline germaphobe. When baby came, we awoke on a little person's terms. We changed messy diapers. We clapped at toilet success. And we enjoyed it so much we did it two more times! We loved the change.

But we don't love all change.

I live in a city with messed up traffic lights. I've tried to make sense of them and cannot. One early morning I approached an intersection and it changed from green to red. I stopped and saw no one else around. I looked at the light and asked "Why? Did you get tired? Did your green need a rest?" Finally, I saw a car approach from my right. Just as it reached the intersection, the light turned red on her. She had to stop, I got to go.

We don't like change that doesn't make sense. We don't like change that reinforces our fear. We don't like change that threatens our worth, belonging or competence.

We love change that moves us toward fulfillment. Some change comes uninvited. What we see initially as a threat may be a gift in clever disguise. It might lead to positive transformation. But if our mindset is "I don't like change" we may never give it the opportunity it deserves.

The difference is in the perspective.

Myth 2: Change is hard.

Change *is* work. Change isn't always easy. But if I believe change is hard, I brace myself. If I believe change is work, I prepare myself.

John Wooden won 10 NCAA basketball championships at UCLA, posted an 88-game winning streak and 24 of his players were named All-America. On the first day of practice, he would teach his players how to put on their socks and shoes. As silly as it sounds, he would explain the most important equipment they had are socks and shoes.

> You play on a hard floor. You must have shoes that fit right. And you must not permit your socks to have wrinkles. Hold up the sock; work it around the little toe area and the heel area. Smooth it out good. Then hold the sock while you put on the shoe. The shoe must be spread apart, not just pulled on the top laces. Tighten it up by each eyelet. Tie it and then double-tie it.

Coach Wooden said he wanted these things done, otherwise they would not have prepared in the best way possible: "It's the little details that make the big things come about."

The Greeks used a word for work that we translate *energy*. Energy births life. Bracing against change feels life-preserving, but it isn't life-giving. Preparing for change is like furnishing a room for the expected baby. We are getting ready.

The difference is in the resistance.

God is the Change Artist. He leads you into change that moves you toward fulfillment. You rally to the change because you want to satisfy deep longings.

There are times people change for the sake of change. They think anything is better than what they have. "Maybe we just need a little change" they say. They are headed for disappointment.

So how do you know what is God-given, God-led change that will satisfy deep longing and what is misguided change? How do you craft what he is shaping?

Start Well Before You Start New

There are too many ideas as to what a great marriage is or what a couple should do. If you don't know what you desire, others will tell you what you should want. True desires are different than what you think you should desire. They are different from what other people think you should desire. They are different from what you pretend to desire when others are watching.

Every couple misses their true and God-given desires when they fall into this pit:

- Popular thought leads to bad thinking.
- Bad thinking leads to wrong focus.
- Wrong focus leads to missing the point.

Have you ever started something and didn't finish? Have you and your partner tried to do something different only to give up? It's likely you followed popular thought into misplaced focus and misdirected energy.

If people start something before there is an environment to sustain it, life expectancy is short. That is why the sun and earth and water came before trees and flowers and animals and people. No environment, no life. It is also why people who win the lottery often have little to show for it within a few years. No environment for financial management, no money. It is also why, according to LiveScience.com, couples who have sex earliest in their relationship had the worst outcomes. Start well before you start new.

Your true desires are the environment in which what you do grows and thrives. You have desires to accomplish: this relates to goals. You have desires to become: this relates to character. You have desires that are quantitative and qualitative. You may want children (quantitative) but you also want them to be well-rounded individuals (qualitative). Desires promote worth, belonging and competence. They enhance your freedom and unity.

Your life is full of clues to your true and God-given desires.

Clue 1: A renowned consultant, Thomas Paterson, developed an evaluation matrix in which he asks four questions: In the areas of your personal growth, family and friends, finance and career, faith and community:

- What is right that you want maximized?
- What is wrong that you want changed?
- What is confusing that you want clarified?
- What is missing that you want added?

The aim of the exercise is to review your answers and look for common themes. Those shine a light on what God is initiating in you and your marriage.

Clue 2: Who has come into your life with positive influence? What is appealing about them? What do they do that intrigues you?

Clue 3: What new opportunities exist? Maybe it's something to participate in or to experience. What is something you thought "I'd like to try that?"

Clue 4: What talents and gifts do you have that are crying for expression? You not only possess the gifts, they are beginning to possess you. They are the whiny child in your room of awesomeness. They want to get out and play.

Clue 5: What networks have you become involved in?

Clue 6: What are your real passions? What do you do that causes you to feel you have come alive?

> Sad is that day for any man when he becomes absolutely satisfied with the life that he is living, the thoughts he is thinking and the deeds he is doing; until there ceases to be forever beating at the door of his soul a desire to do something larger which he seeks and knows he was meant and intended to do. Philipps Brooks

> Hold fast to dreams for if dreams die, life is a broken-winged bird that cannot fly. Langston Hughes

> The faculty to dream was not given to mock us. There is a reality back of it. There is a divinity behind our legitimate desires. Orison Swett Marden

> Death is not the greatest loss in life. The greatest loss is what dies inside us while we live. Norman Cousins

Clue 7: What popular trends do you embrace? What trends do you resist? (Example: Why is your partner embracing fitness? Why are you resisting social media?) What is the desire behind your acceptance or avoidance?

Clue 8: What do you pray about? Prayer is when the heart is most real and vulnerable. We know God knows our heart, so it doesn't do any good to offer fake prayers. What do your prayers tell you about your true desires?

Clue 9: What qualities do you want to characterize you, your marriage and your immediate family? Change isn't just focused on doing but on being.

Clue 10: What beliefs and convictions drive you? A belief is agreement with a statement you believe is true. A conviction is a non-negotiable behavior or attitude that is the basis for decision making. A couple may agree "debt is bad." A conviction says, "We don't carry any debt."

Desires establish your environment for change. You allow and prioritize changes in your marriage based on their harmony with your true desires. Otherwise, you will experience frustration. You will keep trying things that don't work. You will be guessing at what is best for you. You will be spinning wheels in hopes of discovering the more God has for you.

You craft change around five answers:

1. What is the end result? How does this lead to fulfillment? When our desire is satisfied, how will we know?

2. Where are we now in relation to the end? What needs to happen to get there? How long is the road we need to travel and what are some of the mileposts that indicate progress? What is the cost of this change?

3. What obstacles do we need to overcome to reach our destination? What opportunities do we have already in place? (Clues 2-5 may point to some of these).

4. What is the next best move we can make? What can we do now that will give us momentum? What is a small win to encourage us?

5. Who do we need to help us? Is there a coach that can guide us or mentor that can teach us?

Drive to Thrive

Of all the marriages in the Bible, we probably know the most about Abraham and Sarah.

First named Abram, God changed his name to Abraham, which means "father of many". That presented a problem. At the time God changed his name, Abraham was childless and impotent. In Hebrew, names had meaning. So when Abraham would introduce himself to a fellow Hebrew, that person heard Abraham say "Hello, I am Father of Many." To which, of course, a person would ask, "Wow, how many children do you have?"

Abraham *had an identity and nothing to show for it.*

Do you ever feel this way? You have a dream. Your desire is so great you can taste it. You talk of what will be as if it already is; and people just watch and wait to see if it will be.

God believes in you. He believes in your marriage. You have more than a plan. You have promise.

Abraham *had a promise, and no power of his own to fulfill it.*

History says "Against all hope, Abraham in hope believed and so became the father of many nations....Without weakening in his faith, he faced the fact that his body was as good as dead – since he was about a hundred years old – and that Sarah's womb was also dead. Yet he did not waver through unbelief regarding the promise of God, but was strengthened in his faith and gave glory to God, being fully persuaded that God had power to do what he had promised."

You've done the hard work of starting well before starting new. You are convinced the plan in place reflects God's purpose in your life. God will enable!

How did Abraham know the time had come for God to keep his promise? Apparently, one night he and Sarah were home, reclining in their rockers. He started the night impotent. Sarah started the night barren. Abraham looked at his wife. Passion arose. He told her to put in her teeth and take off her clothes.

Like Thomas, you are ready to return and reinvest. Like Abraham and Sarah, you are ready to make new.

Drive means you T.E.A.M with God's power. You take the time, energy, abilities and money he has trusted to you and you infuse it into the areas of change he has called you to.

You no longer order your life around calendar and crisis, urgency or conformity, good ideas and great opportunities. You order it around what you know is true, God-given and fulfilling. You don't take side roads,

popular roads or roads less-travelled. You drive the way that sets you free.
The toll is too great otherwise.

At first, I saw God as my observer, my judge,
keeping track of the things I did wrong,
so as I know whether I merited heaven
or hell when I die.
He was out there sort of like a president.
I recognized His picture when I saw it,
but I really didn't know Him.

But later on
when I met Christ,
it seemed as though life were rather
like a bike ride,

but it was a tandem bike,
and I noticed that Christ
was in the back helping me pedal.

I don't know when it was
that He suggested we change places,
but life has not been the same since.

When I had control,
I knew the way.
It was rather boring,
but predictable...
it was the shortest distance
between two points.

But when He took the lead,
He knew delightful long cuts,
up mountains,
and through rocky places
at breakneck speeds,
it was all I could do to hang on!

Even though it looked like madness,
He said, "Pedal!"

I was anxious
and asked,
"Where are you taking me?"
He laughed and didn't answer,
and I started to learn to trust.
(Anonymous)

The FUN Coach: New

1. Can you think of a time where you missed the point because of wrong focus? What was the thinking behind it? Were you being true to yourselves or following the thoughts and interests of others?

2. Work through the Ten Clues exercise. Take your time. Thorough is better. The first clue is the base for the others. After finishing the first clue, identify common themes between what is right, wrong, confused or missing. Themes might be money related, time and priority related, relational problems, lack of knowledge or direction. This is a very personal exercise. Don't worry about doing it right: just work until it feels complete. List the themes.

3. Match clues 2-8 to your answers: So what people you've met, networks you're involved in, etc. line up with the themes you identified?

4. Which of those themes seem most related to qualities you want for you, your marriage and family?

5. Look at the themes you just listed that match to qualities. Are there any beliefs or convictions about those that you and your partner need to clarify?

6. Take any theme and put it through the next exercise: The five answers that craft change. What was easy about that exercise? What answer is hardest to come by?

7. How aware are you of God being active in your marriage? What can I do to help you further understand his love for you and leading in your life and marriage?

Happy Endings

Our wedding was scheduled for 7:30pm. The pastor suggested we begin on the half-hour so that our marriage started on the upswing. That was in the day when we had clocks with a big hand and a little hand.

I spent the day with a friend from college playing ball but trying not to hurt myself. I had my clothes organized and my time planned to the minute. I even had a fresh bar of soap-on-a-rope waiting for me in the shower.

I spent most of the time at the church walking the hall behind the platform praying and singing. Eventually I walked out on stage, was joined by my groomsmen and waited. My bride appeared and she walked toward me. I considered it a good beginning. The floor was sloped downward. That helped. She stood in front of me and our eyes locked. We were nineteen.

The reception went on longer than we stayed. At our room, I carried her across the threshold. We bowed our knees and prayed, thanking God for the life he had given to us and the moment we were about to experience together. We stood and I slowly undressed the one I had longed to see in all of her natural beauty.

We know a lot more now than we knew then: our first time passed quickly. But it was no less amazing. We eventually slept. I'm not sure what all emotions accompanied our closing eyes. I do know that I awakened with the most remarkable outlook on life.

I have no idea who I would be without her. I'm certain she has carried our marriage and family on petite shoulders and bent knees. Jesus is very fond of her.

In the course of our life, we have learned to champion who the other is more than we have learned to change the things we want to be different. In doing so, we have become more in love than less. My quirks have become solidified charms.

There have been days I never saw when I said I do: days I failed, days that wore her down, days we did not welcome. There have been the great days of our children's birth, days of wild accomplishment, days of dreams realized. As I look back, one thing has been true of every day: happy or sad, laughing or angry, she has been for me. When you see me on my knees, lips moving, it is in prayerful gratitude for this one truth.

Our united front has been assaulted on so many battle fronts I have lost count. Fortunately, they aren't worth counting. The value has been in the character forged, the communication learned and the courage strengthened. We did not stay close because our communication has been good; our communication has been good because we stayed close.

I eat food that is better for me because of her. She likes football because of me. Change is in the little things over a long time. Upon reflection, it seems like no time at all. And that is wisdom for those who are young: at the time, it seems like it will take eternity for something to improve. After the years, you forget much of what it is you wanted to see changed. You long to go back in time if only to stretch time together further. I hear there is no marriage in heaven. I'm hoping we can be bunk mates.

Our romance and sex only gets better. If we keep this up, I'm certain God will script the Song of Songs 2. Sequels can be superior. And we are still making love with delicacies both old and new.

My parents almost made it to their fiftieth anniversary. Less than two months shy, my dad died. He was on the golf course when his aneurism burst. As the ambulance rushed him to the hospital, they said he kept calling out for my mom, his bride. I understand.

I have always taken comfort knowing two things were true when my father passed: he was golfing with his lifelong best friend, and the night before he had made love to his wife, married since they were nineteen. If I must pass before my wife, may it be with but one twist: I will have golfed in the day, and been in bed with her that night sleeping the peace of satisfied desire.

But that day looks to be a ways off. So we await the new still to come, the new that makes us more and the new we can still make in our world. We hope this book has been a start.

> There are three things that are too amazing for me,
> Four that are beyond comprehension:
> The way of an eagle in the sky,
> The way of a snake on a rock,
> The way of a ship on the high seas,
> The way of a man with a woman.

I'm On Your Side...Scoot Over

Sources Referenced and Recommended Reading

Carolyn Evans, *Forty Beads,* Running Press / Perseus Books Group

John Gottman, *The Seven Principles For Making Marriage Work,* Three Rivers Press

Patricia Love, Steven Stosney, *How To Improve Your Marriage Without Talking About It,* Broadway Books

Patricia Love, Jo Robinson, *Hot Monogamy,* Penguin Group

Betsy Prioleau, *Swoon,* W.W. Norton and Company

Chrisianna Northup, Pepper Schwartz, James Witte, *The Normal Bar,* Crown Publishing

Made in the USA
Charleston, SC
23 September 2013